Richard A. Hussian
Ronald L. Davis

Responsive Care
Behavioral Interventions
With
Elderly Persons

Research Press
2612 North Mattis Avenue • Champaign, Illinois 61821

Advisory Editor, Frederick H. Kanfer

Contents

Exhibits

Tables

Preface

Practicing clinicians often must sort through a bewildering array of books, articles, and papers dealing with psychological and behavioral problems of the aged to find any practical help. For this reason, we have written *Responsive Care* specifically for those clinicians and other caregivers who must deal with patients' problem behavior on a daily basis. The text is a practical guide for analyzing and treating behavioral disorders among elderly patients in institutions or under home care.

Our approach, which emphasizes both the analysis of age-related problems and various methods of modifying behavior, lends itself to:

1. Easy application. You will learn how to decrease inappropriate behavior and increase appropriate behavior.
2. Ready accountability. You can draw up contracts with clients and their families to change behavior.
3. Continuous monitoring. You will be able to monitor your client's progress and adjust the treatments to fit particular situations.
4. Application by paraprofessionals and other mediators. Our approach can be used by any health care worker or family member who has been adequately trained in its techniques.
5. Reduced reliance on inferences and value judgments. You will be able to evaluate behavior more objectively, relating symptoms to possible causes such as illness, reactions to drugs, and the like. Patients do not always know their behavior has changed or that they are acting inappropriately as the result of a medication or illness.
6. Focus on less restrictive treatments. The methods we discuss will give you a greater range of choices in treating inappropriate behavior.

Our approach in this book has been used successfully with a variety of elderly populations in various settings. Some of the methods we describe are based on procedures that have been well documented over the years as effective and easily replicated. Other suggestions and techniques have been designed by ourselves or our colleagues at Terrell State Hospital and other settings. In using these protocols, you will need to adapt them to your own situation and monitor the treatment carefully. You should find, however, that the protocols work well in a variety of different conditions and settings.

Although we emphasize behavior analysis and treatment, we also acknowledge the importance of nonbehavioral approaches. We have always incorporated an interest in somatic etiology and treatment in our work with the elderly. However, we feel that all interventions and assessments must be judged according to the criteria used in idiopathic trials. In our estimation, behavior analysis, even when applied to somatic concerns and therapeutic procedures, can provide such accountability.

The programs, protocols, and ideas contained in this book are the result not only of our own efforts but the efforts of countless others. We owe a debt of gratitude to our co-workers, staff, colleagues, and patients.

In particular, we would like to express our deep appreciation for the assistance of the aides, nurses, interns, and social workers on the Geriatric Unit at Terrell State Hospital; Drs. Jacqueline Baumeister and Sioe Tan; the rehabilitation and remotivation staff; Dr. Charles Bridges and Gary Mayhew of the Extended Unit; and our wives and families who gave us support and encouragement during the months of writing.

Our clients, however, have been our most important source of information and have stimulated us to look at old problems in new ways. We hope that the results of our relationship with them will help other mental health professionals improve the lives of their elderly patients.

1
Introduction to the Population

In this chapter, we describe the characteristics of the elderly population with which clinicians often work. It is important to recognize the normal and abnormal changes associated with aging in order to develop the correct assessment, diagnosis, and treatment of behavioral disorders in these clients. Some of our recommendations are based primarily on common sense while others call for substantial modification of protocols to manage various types of geriatric disorders.

Relevant Physical Changes

A variety of physiological changes accompany normal aging and may contribute to inappropriate behavior in the elderly. Identifying these changes is important to the process of assessing behavior and specifying a cause. These changes may also influence the type of intervention chosen, requiring some modifications of standard behavior therapy.

Assessment

Changes in the patients' sensory systems may result in a pattern of abnormal responses similar to those caused by other factors such as brain damage, unfortunate reinforcement history, drug reactions, and the like. Some of the most common sensory changes are:

1. Sight: Visual changes include astigmatism due to corneal changes, loss of vision for short wavelengths (blue-violet range), increased light scatter in the eye, decreased contrast discrimination, and a greater incidence of cataracts.

2. Hearing: Aging affects auditory acuity and discrimination. The person may not only lose the ability to hear softer sounds but may also lose other tones in the auditory range as well.
3. Pain: Sensitivity to pain may decrease in various places in the body.
4. Smell and taste: Often the senses of smell and taste decline, making food less appetizing. The client may smell or taste odors and flavors that have no external source or may also find that the taste or smell of familiar foods and other materials keeps changing.

Because of these changes, elderly clients may appear to be responding independently of normal stimuli (Eastwood & Corbin, 1983; White, 1980). They may void in the wrong location, address a stranger as a friend or relative, suffer burns from touching or holding hot objects, and try to eat inedible items. Such behaviors could be viewed not only as inappropriate but also as symptomatic of some underlying mental disorder. Therefore, understanding the normal processes of sensory loss and decline can lead to a more positive and accurate assessment of the behavior and a correct plan of treatment.

Response times also tend to increase with age, possibly because nerve transmission is impaired, as reflected by a slowed electroencephalogram pattern in many elderly patients. The more information older people are given, the more time they require to process and respond to it correctly. However, a significant change in response times and EEG patterns generally indicates some pathological brain function and not an age-related change per se (Thompson, 1976).

Age also affects the way drugs act in the body. The action of drugs is determined primarily by four processes: absorption, distribution, metabolism, and excretion. All four processes undergo age-related changes; as a result, elderly patients may experience different drug reactions than do younger patients.

Some of the age-related changes that alter the pharmacokinetics of medication include a decreased cardiac output, decreased renal flow, increased fatty tissue, and decreased levels of serum albumin (Hicks, Dysken, Davis, Lesser, Ripeckyj, & Lazarus, 1981). On the whole, these changes result in a lengthier half-life of the medication, that is, the effects of most drugs will last longer when taken by an elderly patient than by a younger person.

The elderly individual may exhibit symptoms that appear to be solely behavioral disturbances when in fact they may be caused by drug reactions. The functional analysis of a problem behavior, then, requires some knowledge of the side-effects of various medications. If a patient exhibits the following behaviors, check for the type and dosage of drugs the patient may be taking.

1. Sedation, lethargy, a general slowing of responses, depression, and psychomotor retardation.
2. Sleep disturbances (due to changes in REM cycle).
3. Excitement (often paradoxically resulting from barbiturate use).
4. Confusion and disorientation.
5. Hallucinations (where none were experienced or reported before).
6. Somatic complaints (constipation, dizziness, blurred vision, urinary retention, tachycardia, dry mouth).
7. Tics and twitches.
8. Anxiety (as manifested by tremors).
9. Ataxia (unsteady gait).
10. Paresthesia (abnormal sensation such as burning, prickling).
11. Skin disorders (rashes, burns, itching, etc.).

The mental health professional should pay careful attention to the elapsed time between the client's ingestion of a medication and the onset of any of these symptoms. Many of the symptoms will occur fairly rapidly—within a matter of hours or days—after the medication has been taken. In many cases, establishing cause and effect between drugs and symptoms is often a matter of simple observation.

Intervention

Age-related changes, which affect the functional analysis of a problem behavior, must also be considered when designing a treatment. Even when the targeted problem is not directly caused by the physical changes described previously, they may still affect the treatment outcome. The mental health professional must be able to design a treatment that will have a reliable and predictable effect on the patient and produce the desired outcome. This includes considering the individual differences of each patient. In a reinforcement program, for example, the available reinforcers would need to be tailored to accommodate the person's physical capabilities and limitations.

The design of treatment programs and facilities can help compensate for the changes in clients' physical abilities. For example, the environment can be structured to reduce glare, limit the use of short wavelength colors, and increase the contrast between important symbols (signs, cues, prompts) and their background (Sullivan, 1983).

In addition, stimulus enhancement and stimulus control training can help strengthen appropriate behaviors by intensifying the desired stimulus. Bright colors, loud auditory cues, clearly marked signposts, and the like can be used to overcome the sensory limitations caused by age-related changes. For example, in teaching clients with progressive dementia to locate a bathroom, clients could be trained to look for a specific color cue on the bathroom door rather than to search for the toilet or bathroom itself. Through intensive training, the client's voiding would gradually come under the control of the color cue instead of the old stimulus, the toilet or bathroom sign.

For stimulus enhancement and control procedures to be effective, however, clients must be able to discriminate the symbol or cue from its background. Bright, long wavelength colors such as red, orange, or yellow can be used against a contrasting background. The symbol or stimulus should also be simple and free from other symbols or cues that could confuse the client or compete with the main symbol. Individual client preferences might also be considered when designing such signs.

Treatment design and delivery can also be affected by drug-related changes in client behavior and functioning. While suggesting adjustments in medication is beyond the scope of this book, the mental health professional can make the following recommendations to a team physician or during consultation.

1. Begin with small doses of medication; increase them only when needed and in the absence of inappropriate side-effects.
2. Manipulate changes in only one medication at a time to avoid interactions between drugs and to help pinpoint the effectiveness or negative side-effects of any particular drug.
3. Closely monitor the frequency, duration, and/or intensity of the target behavior being treated by medication. Notify

the physician if the medication does not appear to affect the behavior. Or, once the behavior is deemed acceptable, suggest reducing the medication.

4. Periodically assess the client for undesirable side-effects while the medication is being taken and notify the physician if these effects appear or intensify.

Changes in Learning Ability and Memory Capacity/Quality

Most studies show significant, though moderate, differences in learning and memory processes between elderly and younger groups. The differences are evident in visual, auditory, and tactile memory (Riege & Inman, 1981; Walsh & Thompson, 1978); recall accuracy and the effectiveness of rehearsal strategies (Sanders, Murphy, Schmitt, & Walsh, 1980); and long-term memory (Bruning, Holzbauer, & Kimberlin, 1975). These age-related differences between the two groups appear to widen when several types of information or instructions are given simultaneously (Erber, Herman, & Botwinick, 1980). However, when elderly individuals are allowed more time to respond or they are trained in various information retrieval strategies, the differences lessen somewhat.

Contrasts in learning between older and younger age groups are often harder to demonstrate. In general, it appears the elderly group seems to take longer to learn items, particularly if the items have little meaning to them. They also tend to change tactics more slowly for learning new material.

Assessment

Accurate assessment of memory functioning and the ability to learn or relearn is crucial in geriatric practice. Deficits in both these functions are among the clearest signs of impaired cognitive ability. Memory tests are probably used more frequently than any other single test of mental status. As a result, they make a greater contribution to the mental health professional's decision-making process than do other types of functional tests.

Unfortunately, even normal, well-functioning elderly individuals can appear to have significant "organic" impairment on many standardized memory tests. This is the case, in part, because the normative samples do not include a proportionate number of elderly people. Such errors can be serious since changes in memory are associated with delirium, dementia, and depression among the elderly, thus making differential diagnosis among these illnesses difficult. Mental health professionals can reduce test errors by changing the procedure of memory testing in the following ways:

1. Avoid using time limits during tests of memory function. Clients should be allowed to demonstrate their capability without adding anxiety as a potential confounding variable. Prompt clients to respond to items as needed, particularly when they hesitate or omit part of a correct response. Keep in mind the guideline often used by neuropsychologists: Permit clients to show whether they know the correct response and do not penalize them for long response times.

2. Slow the testing to allow for full responses to each question and to reduce the client's anxiety. Be sure that an incorrect response is not the result of a client's inability to hear or understand the question.

3. When probing memory function, test the clients on information that is meaningful to them. Nonsense syllables and unrelated lists of items are not retained as well as items familiar to the client. This approach in general is a more ecologically valid test of memory.

4. Follow verbal responses with reinforcement, such as "That's very good." The reinforcement should be delivered for *responding* to the examiner's questions, not simply for *correct* responses. Using this type of reinforcement will encourage clients to answer questions and volunteer information.

Intervention

Intervention techniques need not be modified greatly for clients who show moderate memory decline normally associated with aging. These interventions may consist of writing down instructions, designing a schedule for taking medication, encouraging clients to keep a diary, and other cues which may help increase compliance.

When a client's memory function is significantly impaired, however, special intervention techniques are required. For example:

1. Give frequent prompts immediately before each required task or available activity. Post a calendar of events in a prominent location as well as lists of required tasks, times for bathing, grooming, and the like.

2. If a token economy program is being used, post the token store prices and the amount of points earned for each of the various target responses in a prominent place. A token economy program uses points, chips, slips of paper, or other items as "tokens" awarded for appropriate responses. Tokens can then be cashed in for favorite items or activities. Token slips may have to be fastened to the clothing of some clients to prevent the slips from being misplaced.
   Use stimulus enhancement techniques (see Chapter 5). Simple cues or colors may continue to control various client responses when cognitive mediators fail.
4. Train family members and other caretakers to give clients medication and provide other routine care when it is obvious that clients cannot do so for themselves.
5. Above all, be patient and do not overreact to clients' noncompliance when it is related to deficient memory function. If other symptoms of dementia are evident and the client appears to ignore requests, shouting, pulling, or arguing with the client will not hasten compliance.

Changes in the Clinical Population

In addition to some of the changes already described, elderly individuals may show other characteristics and etiologies not seen as frequently in younger client populations. These problems include depression that manifests differently in the older population, the frequent incidence of physical illnesses which can lead to behavioral disorders, and the relatively high rate of progressive, degenerative diseases that affect brain structure and function.

Depression

The incidence of clinically relevant depression is higher among the elderly than in any other age group. Depression is implicated in the disproportionate number of suicides in this group. This type of age-related depression may be difficult for the mental health professional to detect, particularly if the clinician feels that sadness and low activity levels are "natural" consequences of the aging process.

Another problem in assessing geriatric depression is the nature of standard depression scales. These scales tend to include a number of somatic symptoms such as decreased sexual interest and changes in appetite and sleeping habits. Yet such decreases often accompany the normal aging process. As a result, these changes are less indicative of depression among the aged than in younger age groups. More reliable indicators of depression among elderly people include emotional states such as agitation and apathy when these conditions represent a change from a client's usual behavior.

Alternative depression scales have been developed in an attempt to eliminate the bias in standard scales. Brink and his colleagues have devised a Geriatric Depression Scale in which the norm group is older and more similar to the individuals being tested (Brink, Yesavage, Lum, Heersema, Adey, & Rose, 1982; Yesavage, Brink, Rose, Lum, Huang, Adey, & Leirer, 1983).

Mental health professionals should also be aware of two other important points regarding depression in elderly clients. First, depression often accompanies various physical illnesses and imbalances in older people and may even be the result of medications taken for such ailments. Beta-blocker antihypertensive medication is commonly known to cause depression in many patients. Physical problems that often result in depression include hypokalemia (decreased potassium), anemia, hypothyroidism, Parkinson's disease, and cardiopulmonary insufficiency. Sudden onset of depression, therefore, should be investigated in light of one or more of these conditions or as the result of medication taken for these and other disorders.

Second, depression can occur in a demented client, which would cloud the diagnostic and treatment process even further. Particularly in the early stages of dementia, the client, who may often be aware of what is happening, may become depressed as abilities decline. The clinician must recognize that the depression exists *in addition* to the dementia, since the depression can be treated separately. In fact, relieving the depression may enable the client to demonstrate a higher level of functioning than could be seen previously.

Delirium

Elderly people tend to show both psychological and behavioral symptoms when suffering from acute illnesses or imbalances. While the reason for this close association between physical problems and behavioral disturbances is unclear, it has been reported reliably (Shraberg, 1980). The mental health professional must consider acute organic etiologies whenever a client's behavior changes rapidly, is intense, and involves confusion, disorientation, mania, or depression. The causes of these acute psychological and behavioral disturbances are varied and include those listed in Table 1.1.

In one study, out of 116 patients aged 65 or older admitted to a psychiatric facility, 61.2% had medically caused behavioral problems (Parker, Deibler, Feldshuh, Frosch, Laureana, & Sillen, 1976). These findings suggest that when a clinician encounters a client whose behavioral disturbance appeared rapidly, steps should be taken to rule out an acute physical disturbance *first*. Delirium should also be considered when a client with a progressive dementia suddenly worsens. An abrupt change or exacerbation in symptoms is not typical of the natural progress of a dementing illness, except in the rare event of multi-infarct dementia (dementia caused by strokes). Clues for assessing delirium are presented in Chapter 6.

Dementia

Dementia is a progressive, usually irreversible decline in cognitive, intellectual, language, and memory functions. Approximately 5% to 10% of the elderly population suffer from this condition, although the percentage is much higher among the mentally impaired, institutionalized elderly.

Symptoms of dementia include some combination of the following: confusion, disorientation, inappropriate voiding, self-stimulation, wandering, shadowing (following other people), poor memory, aphasia, agitation, depression, pica (eating inedible objects), furniture relocation, and lack of judgment. In most cases, the onset of dementia is slow and insidious. As a result, many clients can cover up their deficits for some time after the symptoms first appear.

Alzheimer's disease constitutes the majority of progressive dementia cases (70%), while multiple strokes account for much of the remaining 30%. Alzheimer's disease appears to involve a buildup of neurofibrillary tangles and plaques in the brain, causing gradual loss of memory and functioning. The problem for the mental health professional is diagnosing dementia in the absence of any definitive diagnostic tools or tests.

Although several scales have been designed to diagnose organic impairment caused by dementing illnesses (e.g., Reisberg, Ferris, DeLeon, & Crook, 1982; Winogrond & Fisk, 1983), they are not foolproof. Assessment of dementia is still a process of

TABLE 1.1
REVERSIBLE CAUSES OF
COGNITIVE IMPAIRMENT (DELIRIUM)

Medications
 Anti-depressants (Davies, Tucker, Harrow, & Detre, 1971)
 Anti-inflammatories
 Atropine substances
 Bromides
 Cimetidine
 Diuretics
 L-dopa
 Propanolol (Cummings, Benson, & LoVerne, 1980)
 Psychoactives (e.g., McAllister, Scowden, & Stone, 1978)
 Steroids

Metabolic disturbances
 Dehydration (Seymour, Henschke, Cape, & Campbell, 1980)
 Hemodialysis
 Hypercalcemia
 Hypocalcemia
 Hypokalemia
 Hyponatremia
 Uremia

Other
 Addison's disease
 Anaesthesia
 Anemia
 Bacterial and viral infections
 Cardiac arrhythmia
 Congestive heart failure
 Hepatic encephalopathy (Freeman & Rudd, 1982)
 Hyperglycemia
 Hypoglycemia
 Hyperthyroidism
 Hypothyroidism (Portnoi, 1980)
 Metal toxicity
 Pain associated with:
  cholecystitis
  diverticulitis
  endocarditis (Task Force, 1980)
  fractures
  impaction
 Pulmonary failure
 Serum hyperviscosity (Mueller, Hotson, & Langston, 1983)
 Thiamine deficiency
 Trauma
 Tumors
 Vascular insufficiency

ruling out other disorders and observing the client for signs that can be highly correlated with Alzheimer's disease.

From a behavioral perspective, the underlying disease process, once identified, is relatively unimportant. The goal of treatment is to manage the client's deficits and excesses regardless of the cause. If an underlying, treatable cause is present, a somatic intervention is appropriate. If such causes have been ruled out, the clinician's task is then to reduce the management problem(s) related to client behavior. In subsequent chapters, these management problems will be discussed in more detail and assessment and treatment guidelines offered.

At this point, we would like to summarize the recommendations made in this chapter based on the characteristics of the elderly population we have described.

Recommendations for Assessment

1. The assessor's guiding principle should be to assume that the client's problem is due to a *reversible* cause or condition rather than to an irreversible one. Only after ruling out every conceivable possibility should the mental health professional consider an irreversible cause for the problem.
2. Learn to recognize the signs of delirium and to interpret laboratory values (see Exhibit 6.6 in Chapter 6). Learn the diseases and imbalances that correlate with cognitive and behavioral impairment. Such knowledge is important even when a progressive dementia is present. An accurate assessment and treatment of delirium and depression can enable clients to recover some functioning even when they are chronically organically impaired.
3. Be alert for signs of a progressive dementia that are less well known but as predictive of the disease's progress as well-known symptoms. These indicators include self-stimulation or stereotypy, anomia and other language disorders, signs of inappropriate stimulus control, and furniture relocation.
4. Evaluate the quality of clients' sensory systems. The importance of tests for visual, auditory, and other sensory impairment cannot be overstated.
5. Evaluate and monitor the side-effects of clients' medications throughout the time the drugs are administered— not simply during the initial interview or when the medication is first ingested.

6. Use time-sampling procedures to assess the frequency, duration, and intensity of problem behaviors in lieu of standardized evaluation tools. Time sampling can produce more accurate assessments and analysis of behavior than many standardized instruments and can be used conveniently throughout treatment.

7. If standardized tests are used, break up the testing time to avoid tiring clients and introducing a negative bias into the process. Give instructions clearly and (whenever possible) allow sufficient time for the client to respond. Getting some kind of response from the elderly client is more important than adhering to strict time limits.

8. Use active probing during the initial interview and do not rely on spontaneous replies. Prompt and reinforce the client's responses frequently to avoid problems posed by errors of omission.

9. Use other sources of information besides the client's own report. Outside verification of what the client says is crucial in determining the onset and symptoms of a disorder which appeared before the client's first contact with the evaluator.

Recommendations for Treatment

1. For clients with moderate to severe cognitive dysfunction, use color coding freely, particularly from the longer wavelengths (red, orange, yellow). These color codes can be used to mark rooms according to their function, tag client property, and guide clients to areas they may have trouble locating.

2. Engage more than one of the client's senses in any attempt to use prompting, shaping, or reinforcement. Many elderly clients experience a decline in sensory systems normally associated with aging or may suffer significant deterioration caused by disease or drug side-effects. As a result, they may need to *see* as well as *hear* instructions or cues. For instance, a verbal prompt to attend a scheduled activity might be accompanied by a flashing light to cue the hearing impaired client.

3. In general, prompts should be of a higher intensity than those used with younger clients.

4. For problems of stimulus control, use the stimulus enhancement and stimulus control procedures outlined in Chapter 5. These programs attempt to shape different responses in different settings and are not merely response reduction techniques. In some cases, the goal is not to eliminate a client response but simply to relocate it.

5. The shortened attention span of clients with moderate to severe cognitive impairment in delirium and dementia can be used to help avert some management problems such as combativeness, exit-seeking (attempts to leave the facility), and furniture relocation. Such patients are often easily distracted from one activity or behavior to another. The emphasis is on preventing the unfortunate consequences of problem behavior rather than intervening after the client has become a serious problem or caused an incident.

6. Primary reinforcers should be considered for use in shaping procedures with moderately to severely impaired clients. Primary reinforcers are items such as food, liquids, and the like that can satisfy some physical need immediately. Secondary reinforcers must be traded for primary reinforcers to be valued. Although secondary reinforcers should be tried first because they are more natural, clients in the latter stages of a progressive dementia often have difficulties understanding and using token slips or social reinforcement. On the other hand, primaries may be faded out and secondary reinforcement substituted if clients show improvements in their level of functioning and if discharge is imminent. This method is typically used with clients whose underlying problems have acute organic causes that have been treated successfully.

7. A continuous reinforcement schedule should be devised when attempting to shape responding by clients with severe cognitive dysfunction. Shaping behavior involves training a component of a behavior at the start and gradually adding more components until the end-point behavior is exhibited. Attempts to retrain clients to feed or groom themselves may be successful only if a reinforcer is delivered each time the targeted response occurs. Usually the overall goal, such as combing their own hair, must be broken down into smaller goals: grasping the comb, bringing the comb to the hair, pulling it through the hair, and the

like. Each smaller goal must be followed by a positive reinforcer.

In the next chapter, we introduce behavior therapy techniques that can be applied to many of the behavioral disturbances shown by impaired elderly patients. Keep in mind the population characteristics described in this chapter when reading the assessment and treatment procedures. Also consider the many individual differences you are likely to encounter among clients in a mental health practice. These differences will affect the design and application of various techniques discussed in this book.

2

Behavior Management

Behavioral assessment and behavior therapy have been used successfully to change a variety of target behaviors from phobias, cigarette smoking, bed-wetting and defecating to more difficult conditions such as irrational thoughts, depression, and some types of schizophrenia. The behavioral approach is no longer identified solely with operant conditioning, aversive programs, and systematic desensitization. It now encompasses modification of cognitive events as targets and incorporates social variables in group therapy. *Behavior therapy* or *management*, as used in this book, includes any intervention that attempts to change the frequency, intensity, duration, or location of a specific behavior or set of behaviors through systematically varying antecedent stimuli or consequential events.

Prior to intervention, a definition of treatment targets is needed. *Behavioral assessment* involves attempts to identify a client's problem responses in terms of their nature, frequency, intensity, duration, and location which may be measured before, during, and after intervention. Behavioral assessment does not take into consideration underlying psychodynamisms or events in the client's past that are not represented in the person's present environment.

Thus, the behavior therapy or management described in this book is based on the principles of learning and conditioning, such as reinforcement, contiguity, avoidance, and modeling, which have been validated in controlled settings and are thought to apply in other settings as well. In this approach we assume that all behavior, whether deemed appropriate or inappropriate, follows these principles. Generally, the appropriateness of a behavior is determined by the context in which it occurs and the value judgments of the observer(s).

15

Behavior in a Context

The behavioral approach analyzes particular behaviors in terms of their relationship to other events. Events that occur prior to the behavior are known as *antecedents* while those that follow the behavior are termed *consequences*. These events form the context for the behavior studied and help maintain it.

The observed behavior, then, is always viewed within a given setting. We can say that behavior is an *operant*; that is, a response to internal or external stimuli. An operant view stresses the relationship between these events (antecedents and consequences) and the rate, intensity, duration, and nature of the observed behavior.

The emphasis in behavioral assessment and therapy has been focused primarily on the relationship between *observable* events. However, no understanding of geriatric behavior would be complete without considering *nonobservable* events or events that are not readily observable which may elicit overt behavior. These internal factors then interact with the environment to produce behaviors that a caretaker can observe.

Internal events fall into two categories: (1) those that cannot be measured (such as hallucinations) and (2) those that can be measured but require special devices not usually available at the time the behavior is observed (for example, hyperglycemia). From a behavioral point of view, the clinician is most interested in observable behavior (such as talking to one's self), which can be monitored to determine the effectiveness of an intervention.

Thus, we can view behavior—appropriate and inappropriate—as the result of an interaction between internal events and a variety of external events. For example, a client may strike out at others when the noise level on a ward becomes aversive (observable stimulus) or when suffering from the delusion that others are persecuting him (nonobservable stimulus). Clients may also attack others if the behavior has resulted in reinforcing consequences in the past, such as getting something they have wanted. The reinforced behavior is also more likely to occur when other, more appropriate behaviors do not get the same results. Internal and external factors can be present in varying degrees, producing behaviors of different duration, intensity, nature, and rate even within the same person at different times.

Behavior in geriatric settings is evaluated in the same way as behavior exhibited in other settings. Careful attention to context and to less readily observed variables is essential in understanding, predicting, and controlling clients' behavior.

Most types of behavior are acceptable unless they occur in excess (too long or at too high an intensity) or at the wrong time and place. Caretakers expect a minimum amount of other behaviors from elderly clients such as participating in activities, getting out of bed during the day, and grooming themselves. When these latter types of behavior occur at a rate below the caretaker's expectations, the caretaker naturally becomes concerned. As a result, the decision to intervene is based upon two more variables: the client's rate of response and the observer's criteria for what constitutes acceptable behavior.

The context in which a behavior occurs and the caretaker's expectations become even more important when a behavior happens at an appropriate rate but at the wrong time and/or place. Such behaviors are best viewed as the result of poor stimulus control. That is, the normal stimulus-response sequence is absent and another sequence has taken its place. While it could be argued that most inappropriate behaviors are the result of poor stimulus control, certain target behaviors are more striking examples of this phenomenon. They include urinating in the wrong place, public sexual behavior, wandering into dangerous areas, coming into contact with dangerous objects such as heated stove tops and bath water, and constantly moving furniture. These behaviors occur fairly frequently in an elderly population.

When poor stimulus control is determined as the maintaining factor in an inappropriate behavior, intervention would probably involve both manipulating contextual cues and applying consequences after the behavior occurs. The goal would be to have the behavior occur in an appropriate location or at the proper time rather than to reduce or increase the *rate* of the behavior. This approach not only frees the clinician from having to make difficult decisions concerning the desirability of a particular behavior but also permits intervention at the antecedent level. Changes in cues, prompts, or other environmental stimuli can help a client alter a particular behavior so that it is more correct within a given context. This approach eliminates the need to intervene after an inappropriate response occurs. The emphasis is on changing the context of the behavior, not the behavior itself.

The Importance of Antecedent Control

Woods (1983) describes the manipulation of precedent stimuli to modify behavior within a context as "intervention facilitation." In his work with stereotypy in autistic children, he has manipulated the S^d (stimulus in which the following response is reinforced) and/or the $S^\triangle$ (stimulus in which the following response is not reinforced) to establish stimulus control. The clinician does not have to determine whether a behavior is appropriate, desirable, or deviant, only whether it takes place in the presence of the appropriate stimulus.

The basic principle of antecedent control is that a behavior which occurs at a given frequency in one setting may be appropriate while in another setting the same behavior would be met with aversive consequences. For example, urinating in a reasonably concealed toilet designed for men or women is acceptable. However, the same behavior is likely to provoke serious consequences if it is performed in the middle of a dinner party next to the hostess's chair. The individual will suffer social ostracism, and may even be arrested for committing a misdemeanor. Similarly, ambulating within a secured courtyard is a harmless, appropriate activity, even if the person is gesturing oddly or walking in a somewhat strange manner. But if the same behavior takes place in the middle of a busy highway, the consequences could be fatal for the individual.

Mental health professionals, by viewing behavior in terms of its context, can reduce the possibility of making serious clinical errors. For instance, they may attempt to decrease or eliminate a behavior that is, by itself, not inappropriate and thereby deprive the client of an important and necessary response.

Antecedent control is important for another reason. Preventing inappropriate behavior is usually more desirable than trying to apply consequences after the behavior has occurred. Also, some behaviors are dangerous, and prevention is the only ethically and legally defensible intervention. For example, extreme physical aggression toward others or serious self-abuse must be controlled by prevention whenever possible rather than by intervention after an episode has occurred.

Preventive techniques should be derived from the careful analysis of literature reports and the patterns of inappropriate behavior in each setting. Stimuli that commonly provoke extreme behavior should be eliminated. These include high noise levels, crowding, insufficient privacy, lack of storage space, heavy movable objects that can be used as weapons, and unmarked or hidden areas where behaviors can occur unobserved. However, caretakers should also be alert for less obvious stimuli. For example, careful analysis of a client's aggression pattern may reveal that only one person is the target of the client's behavior. Moving the client to another room or ward might be enough to reduce the frequency of episodes without the need for more intrusive interventions.

Antecedent or stimulus control is also generally safer than attempting to intervene after a dangerous behavior has occurred. Managing aggressive behavior can be risky for the interveners, particularly during or immediately after an episode. When prevention of the behavior is emphasized, other people in the same area are usually at less risk. Also, the behavior can be controlled even when no staff member is present to intervene.

Behavior management techniques that stress *proactive* prevention generally are more desirable than *reactive* intervention. Ideally, the only time post-response intervention should be used is when the controlling stimuli for a particular client are either internal or have not been identified.

Behavioral Model versus Medical Model in Geriatrics

The behavioral model for geriatrics, as proposed by Birren (1970), and revised by Baltes and Barton (1977) and Hoyer (1975) into the biobehavorial model, differs in many ways from the traditional medical model. The differences are primarily in methods of assessment, evaluation of treatment efficacy, and philosophy, as listed in Table 2.1.

The list is not meant to be exhaustive nor represent all practitioners from either model. However, these differences are most likely to surface when a ward or unit within an institution is being reoriented from a medical model to a behavioral one (Hussian, 1981).

Practitioners of behavior therapy are likely to encounter several common misconceptions about behavior management held by individuals trained in another system. These misconceptions include the belief that behavior management is synonymous with psychosurgery; covers only aversive conditioning; demeans the client; asks too much of the elderly patient; works only with animals, the retarded, or children; and cannot work with chronic clients or those functioning at a low level of competence. The practitioner should be aware of these misconceptions and work to overcome them.

For several reasons, the geriatric population tends to be exposed relatively more frequently to the traditional medical

TABLE 2.1
DIFFERENCES BETWEEN
BEHAVIORAL AND MEDICAL MODELS

Behavioral model	*Medical model*
Assessment	
1. Observable behavior is target for change.	1. Observable behavior reflects underlying pathology only.
2. Assessment across time and settings made when possible.	2. Pathology set, so only one measurement necessary.
3. Problem described in specific terms.	3. Problem described in global, nosological terms.
Treatment	
1. Manipulates environmental contingencies.	1. Manipulates internal events through physical mediators.
2. Stresses relearning and rehabilitation.	2. Stresses immediate reduction of symptomology.
3. Relies on continuous data collection for evaluation.	3. Relies on staff's informal observations of change.
4. When approved, may use *contingent* restraint.	4. When needed, uses *preventive* restraint.
Philosophy in practice	
1. Relies on reliable and valid reports of new treatment.	1. Relies on clinical judgment and similar cases in the past.
2. Stresses problem can be modified and reversed despite age.	2. Views problem behavior as naturally occurring with age.

approach than do other age groups. It may be that non-medical practitioners are reluctant to work with elderly patients, that behaviorists lack knowledge of organic etiology, that there is an absence of third-party support for the work of other practitioners, or that elderly clients hesitate to seek help from a mental health professional and instead rely on physicians.

As a result, although medical/psychiatric practitioners are most likely to see elderly mentally impaired clients, this population is still underserved. Even when contact is made, the elderly psychiatrically disabled client may be overlooked. For example, a study conducted by Rabins, Lucas, Teitelbaum, Mark, and Folstein (1983) reviewed consultation use patterns of 651 admissions at Johns Hopkins in 1978. They reported that while clients age 60 or above filled 28.5% of the inpatient beds, only 21.0% of all psychiatric referrals were from this age group. In addition, consultations with elderly clients (age 60+) were 39.0% below the number of consultations with patients aged 45 or younger.

Differences between a medical and behavioral view on aging are often most striking within the nursing profession. In practice, the behavioral treatment programs often rely on nursing staff to collect data, intervene consistently, aid in assessing management problems, and help in program evaluation. As a result, the principles and techniques of behavior therapy should be carefully introduced to gain the cooperation of nursing staff. Nurses should understand clearly how the new model will affect the work they do and what benefits they and their patients can expect to gain from adopting the new model.

If behavior therapy is not introduced sensitively, there are apt to be problems between the nursing staff and mental health professionals. Nurses may feel the data-gathering methods used in the behavioral model are intrusive and burdensome, demeaning to patients, and adding to the work load of nursing staff. Goals and objectives of the behavioral model should be explained in detail and linked to benefits for the nursing staff and client population. While there are likely to be some initial problems in changing from a medical to a behavioral model, the practitioners introducing the new system must work to create open and clear lines of communication. Problems are easier to handle at the beginning of the process than when they have become a source of serious conflict, often leading to a breakdown in communication. Chapter 6 provides some guidelines to overcome initial resistance to the behavioral model in inpatient settings.

For decades, there has been little attention paid to a psychodynamic model of geriatric care. Although one publication, the *Journal of Geriatric Psychiatry*, reports on psychiatric problems and treatment of elderly clients, there is little else in this literature addressing geriatric psychopathology or management. Since Freud, psychoanalytic practitioners have considered elderly personalities as "crystalized" and their pathology difficult if not impossible to change. One such practitioner (Philippopoulos, 1979) wrote that no psychodynamic formulation of elderly psychiatric disorders is possible since older people present "no specified dynamic factors." In other words, the prevalent view has been that elderly people are rigidly fixed in their behavior and little can be done to change them. The incidence of brain impairment, decline in psychosexual forces, and low rate of verbalization among elderly patients may reinforce this view and make practitioners reluctant to work with the geriatric population.

Geriatrics and the Behavioral Model

Many researchers have pointed out the benefits of matching the techniques of a behavioral approach to the specialized problems of the aged (e.g., Birren, 1970; Hoyer, 1973; MacDonald, 1978; McClannahan & Risley, 1975). There are many reasons for such a match, having to do with the nature of the population, the type of target behaviors frequently encountered, and the characteristics of the health care system.

1. The standard operating procedures and policies in most institutions call for well-organized record-keeping systems. Usually the record-keeping system documents some type of problem definition, goals of treatment, and strategies to achieve the goals. Such statements and goals must be written in specific language with measurable and quantifiable terms. The behavioral approach is in keeping with this need and stresses specification of targets and goals, systematic observation, and avoidance of jargon.

2. Outside regulatory and peer review agencies require that these problems, goals, and strategies be free of diagnostic labeling. The behavioral approach also de-emphasizes classification schemes and elaborate diagnostic labels.

3. Referral problems found among most of the elderly population involve specific complaints of excessive or deficient behavior. Generally, older clients do not exhibit personality disorders, free-floating anxiety, and inadequate personalities. As a result, the most appropriate interventions are those designed to address specific management problems. Rehabilitation of target deficits or excesses is a primary feature of behavior therapy.

4. Many clients are referred to inpatient settings because specific behavior problems make it difficult to keep the elderly person at home. These problems include making too much noise, refusing medication, urinating inappropriately, or wandering away. A treatment is needed that can alleviate the problem and return the client home without the need for personality restructuring or achieving insight into personal problems or disorders. A major part of such treatment involves the behavior therapy approach of

restructuring the home environment in order to continue home care.

5. Lengthy therapy for elderly patients is impractical because of the lack of mental health professionals available to work with elderly clients and the resulting high client-to-therapist ratio. Short-term intervention and the extensive use of mediators are hallmarks of the behavioral approach. Most of the behavioral techniques discussed in this book have been carried out by staff aides and family members. The mental health professional provides the treatment design and is available for consultation.

6. Most therapies offered geriatric clients, particularly in institutional settings, can be provided by those who are not psychologists. The most widespread therapies are chemotherapy and rehabilitation activities. A nonmedical, nonrehabilitation specialist must possess skills complementing these two approaches. For example, data collection, measurement, and statistical analyses, all part of the behavioral approach, also can help validate clients' drug therapies. Likewise, rehabilitation programs can be more successful when the activities offered are designed to fit clients' specific needs and are accompanied by sound reinforcement programs. Specifying target responses and designing reinforcement programs are an important part of the behavioral approach.

Special Considerations

Before presenting techniques to assess and treat specific behavior disorders, there are several special considerations regarding geriatric work that need to be discussed. Mental health professionals who have decided to enter geriatrics or to work with elderly clients should be aware of these issues in order to avoid potential pitfalls in their work.

First, move slowly when beginning to counsel elderly clients in an inpatient setting or when establishing a behavior treatment program on a ward or unit. At the outset, train staff, design treatment programs, and collect baseline data on small groups or on single wards and not on larger units. Resistance to new methods is common, and a good first impression can help overcome an initial lack of cooperation on the part of staff and clients. Staff attitudes are best changed by demonstrating how troublesome client behavior can be modified successfully. This approach can be accomplished best by working with small groups of clients and selected staff as mediators. Collected data and word of mouth reports about successful behavior therapy should make subsequent steps much easier to implement.

Second, clinicians should clarify the amount of control and authority they have over the implementation of behavioral programs. Even if the novice clinician is fortunate enough to have the support of the entire staff, turnover rates for staff workers are high and policy changes frequent. Make sure that lines of authority and methods of securing employee cooperation are clearly defined. Supervision of staff should rest, in part, with the program designer, and the ability to influence the behavior of mediators should be negotiated early.

Third, the clinician should become familiar with organic conditions that correlate with inappropriate behavior. Such information is not usually a part of most mental health professionals' training, and it is essential to correct this deficiency. Doing so can improve communication with medical personnel and help prevent loss of time and application of the wrong treatment that can result from an incorrect diagnosis of a client's problem. The clinician must be aware of drug actions, side-effects, and interactions; behavioral and physical correlates of electrolyte disturbances; and common age-related physical diseases. Also, some knowledge of neuropsychological test batteries and their interpretation is valuable.

Fourth, an accurate and complete data collection system must be established and maintained. The system should provide enough information to analyze antecedents and consequences yet be designed so that ward personnel or family members can gather and record the data easily. The amount of writing required should be held to a minimum without sacrificing pertinent information. In most institutions, similar information may also have to be documented in the client's individual record. However, the data collection system rather than the client's record should be used to evaluate programs and make decisions regarding an individual client's progress. (A sample data recording form is presented in Chapter 6, Table 6.2.)

Two final points apply to mental health professionals themselves. First, they should carefully evaluate their criteria for acceptable client behavior. Periodic evaluations should include their expectations for the ultimate goal of a therapeutic intervention and what constitutes progress toward that goal. Often, a clinician must be satisfied with small gains over long time periods and with less ambitious discharge goals. The objective may be simply to discharge the client to a less restrictive setting (e.g., from an inpatient hospital to a rest home). Or it may be to reduce the number of sores on the back of a terminally ill client.

Second, the mental health worker should guard against the attitudes that advanced age equals lack of flexibility in behavior or that age alone sets limits on treatment goals. These attitudes limit client progress and place elderly impaired clients at a distinct disadvantage compared with clients of other ages. Should clinicians find themselves developing such beliefs, they can take two corrective actions: (1) carefully analyze their methods against more successful techniques and (2) spend time with fully functioning people who just happen to be older.

Before proceeding to the next chapter, the reader should become familiar with the terms and definitions listed below. The terms will be used throughout the book, and they form part of the basic vocabulary of the behavioral model.

1. *Correction:* A response reduction procedure which involves requiring the person to restore the environment to its original state before the inappropriate behavior occurred.
2. *Differential reinforcement of other behavior:* A procedure that provides positive reinforcement of an appropriate behavior which replaces an inappropriate behavior.
3. *Extinction:* A technique designed to reduce the likelihood of an inappropriate behavior occurring. Generally the technique involves withholding positive reinforcement until the appropriate behavior occurs.
4. *Overcorrection:* A method of response reduction that requires the person to restore not only the immediate environment but also a larger area following a damaging behavior.
5. *Positive practice:* Prompting a client to engage in the correct series of responses following an inappropriate behavior.
6. *Prompting:* Cueing a client through a gesture, word, or other type of signal to elicit a specified response.
7. *Response cost:* Removing a reinforcement after an inappropriate behavior has occurred. The behavior "costs" the client something.

8. *Restitution:* Requiring one client to reimburse another after taking a personal item. Restitution can also be used in the same manner as correction.

9. *Restriction:* Prohibiting a client from engaging in an activity or receiving a favored item after an inappropriate behavior has occurred.

10. *Seclusion:* A nonbehavioral procedure that involves isolating a client following an inappropriate behavior. In a behavioral approach, seclusion should be used only after a client has refused time out.

11. *Selective reinforcement:* Simultaneously using extinction after inappropriate response(s) and delivering positive reinforcement for desirable response(s).

12. *Shaping:* A procedure that uses reinforcement, prompting and guidance to build up component responses leading to a complete, appropriate behavior.

13. *Stimulus control:* Establishing a strong relationship between an identifiable stimulus (external or internal) and a particular behavior that occurs each time the stimulus is present.

14. *Stimulus enhancement:* Increasing the intensity or contrast of a stimulus to increase appropriate stimulus control.

15. *Time out:* Withholding positive reinforcement after an inappropriate response by removing the client to an area that is isolated or devoid of most natural reinforcers.

16. *Tokens:* A type of secondary reinforcement used to increase desirable client responses. Tokens can take the form of initials or signatures on a card, hole punches, poker chips, or other objects. They can be cashed in for various types of positive reinforcers.

Keep these considerations and terms in mind when reading through the remainder of the book. The following chapters offer guidelines for assessing and treating a variety of disorders found among elderly clients. The disorders are classified as behavioral deficits, excesses, and problems stemming from insufficient or inappropriate stimulus control. We have included special guidelines for those interested in using behavior change techniques with institutionalized clients and outpatients, or in teaching the methods to families of elderly clients.

3

Assessment and Treatment of Behavioral Deficits

Those who care for elderly clients—families and staff of institutions—often have first-hand experience of behavioral deficits in older people. Indeed, one has only to walk through the halls of a nursing home or geropsychiatric facility to see evidence of such deficits in many elderly residents. Some may be in the lobby or dayroom sitting alone watching TV or simply staring into space. In the rooms, staff workers may be spoonfeeding residents who cannot feed themselves, or cleaning up after a patient who has spilled food or drink on himself or on the floor. Some deficits may not be as obvious, for example, the resident in a wheelchair who refuses to walk even though she is perfectly healthy or the person afraid to ask for assistance for fear the staff will label him a nuisance or a troublemaker.

Compounding the problem is the attitude of many caregivers that these deficits are merely a normal part of the aging process. LeBray (1979) cited a survey of nursing home staff that revealed these caretakers regarded depression, incontinence, complaining, confusion, and disorientation as appropriate behavior for elderly clients. Yet such behaviors are not appropriate or normal at any age and often can be treated and reversed. Unfortunately, treatment may not be provided in many cases, partly because staff and families know little about the organic and environmental factors that may trigger or cause such deficits.

Yet attending to behavioral deficits in elderly clients is important for a number of reasons. First, these deficits may occur secondary to a medical disorder such as drug toxicity, metabolic disease, systemic illness, or electrolyte imbalance (Hussian, 1981). Such disorders usually are reversible with timely interventions. If they are ignored, they can cause permanent structural damage in the elderly person.

Second, intervention can counteract the reinforcement of behavioral deficits within an institutional setting. For example, dependent behaviors in an institutionalized population are often deemed acceptable. The elderly nursing home resident is viewed by staff as being sick and in need of help. However, the method of helping, which often involves performing tasks for the resident, may increase dependence on the staff. The cycle perpetuates itself and reinforces the deficits rather than reduces them.

For example, Barton, Baltes, and Orzech (1980) investigated staff encouragement or discouragement of independent behavior in nursing home residents. They found that even though residents behaved independently in the presence of staff, the staff tended to reinforce dependent behavior. Also, residents who engaged in self-motivated behavior were seldom rewarded by staff workers for their efforts. The absence of reinforcement for self-initiated behavior and the reinforcement of dependent behavior can exacerbate already existing deficits. These tendencies have been observed in caregivers who work with both geriatric patients (Lowenthal & Zilli, 1969) and with chronic mental patients offered only custodial care (Paul, 1969).

A third reason for attending to behavioral deficits is that they may be related to a psychological disorder. Depression is the most common psychological disorder of the elderly (Feldman & Lopez, 1982) and depression in the elderly differs in many ways from the depression that is found in younger people. It may not be readily diagnosed by mental health practitioners who are more familiar with the depressive symptoms of a younger population. For example, the elderly depressed tend to present more somatic complaints than their younger counterparts and fewer complaints about dysphoria or sadness. They may also appear to be more confused and disoriented regarding time, date, and place—symptoms that are often viewed as indicators of progressive dementia rather than depression.

Given the importance of assessing and treating behavioral deficits in the elderly, this chapter addresses the issue from the perspective of behavior therapy. Behavioral techniques can provide appropriate interventions in treating deficits among the elderly for several reasons.

First, elderly clients may be cognitively impaired. Their decreased concentration, lack of attention, increased confusion, and disorientation would make it difficult to use a strictly verbal approach in solving behavioral problems. Second, behavioral techniques can be used by paraprofessional staff. These staff are more likely to be intervenors since they are responsible for the direct care of elderly residents in many settings. Third, the kinds of problems commonly encountered, such as incontinence, diminished activity level, and deficits in self-care skills, typically have been treated in a more directive manner, similar to the approach used in behavior therapy.

In the following sections, we look at specific behavioral deficits and different ways of assessing and treating them using the behavioral model.

Increasing Group Activity Attendance

A reduced level of activity has been associated with a number of physiological problems in the elderly population, including vasomotor instability and labile blood pressure (Bonner, 1969). In contrast, a positive relationship exists between an increased level of activity and feelings of well-being (Jeffers & Nichols, 1961). Also, increasing an individual's overall rate of responding has been one component in treating depression (Ferster, 1965). This technique would seem particularly appropriate for a geriatric population with its higher incidence of depression and physiological decline, both of which may be aggravated by diminished activity.

Several studies have been conducted on increasing group activity as a way to raise the overall level of activity among nursing home and psychogeriatric residents. McClannahan and Risley (1975) compared the level of participation in group activities under three conditions:

1. Equipment and materials provided and residents prompted to participate.
2. Equipment and materials not provided.
3. Equipment and materials provided but available only upon request.

They found that when materials and equipment were provided, prompting residents to participate more than tripled the mean percentage of those who became involved with the materials.

McClannahan and Risley (1974) also compared the impact of three different kinds of prompts on the level of attendance at various activities. They discovered that any kind of prompt (P.A. announcements, large print signs, and the like) increased activity attendance and the instances of residents helping one another. During 27 sessions, they recorded 44 instances of one resident helping another to an activity.

Assessing Environmental Variables

Environmental conditions should be assessed before instituting any group activities program. The mental health professional should seek to identify and analyze the antecedents and consequences of residents' behavior that might increase the chances of getting residents to attend the programs and of maintaining their attendance over the life of the program.

Environmental conditions to be assessed include:

1. Structural barriers to wheelchairs and walkers.
2. Distance barriers.
3. Prompts and cues indicating where and when activities are to take place.
4. Furniture type and arrangement within the activity area.
5. Lighting.
6. Content of activities and materials used.
7. Scheduling conflicts.

Although most nursing homes and geropsychiatric facilities are careful to remove structural barriers for residents, some barriers may remain even after thoughtful planning. In addition, while a structural or distance barrier may not preclude attendance at first, it may do so over time. Residents may come to feel it requires too much effort to attend the activity.

Activities should be held in a centrally located area rather than on a wing of a facility. All residents will then have the same distance to travel and the same opportunity to attend the activities. The staff planning the program should walk to the area from different locations to make sure there are no obvious or unrecognized barriers along the route. Staff may even travel the distance in a wheelchair or with a walker to simulate the conditions of some residents who would be prompted to attend the activity.

Prompts and cues are another environmental condition affecting activity attendance. The person conducting activities should first identify the methods already used to communicate with a facility's residents. For example, does the staff use bulletin boards or other places to post announcements? Some facilities may have an intercom system with a loudspeaker. Others may establish times and places when residents are gathered to hear announcements. Are there staff or volunteers who usually deliver messages and items to residents?

If one or more of these communication methods are already in place, they may provide more stimulus control than would a new system. However, the planner should carefully evaluate existing methods of communication to eliminate those that do not work. For example, if a bulletin board is crowded with announcements, a written notice of an activity will be difficult to read, particularly for those with visual problems. A loudspeaker system may be audible in a central location but not in more remote parts of the facility. In addition, residents with a hearing impairment may not be able to understand the announcements. If staff or volunteers are used to deliver notices of activities to residents, they must be reliable (will they deliver the announcements?) and consistent (will they deliver the notices regularly and on time?). Announcements should be delivered to all residents far enough ahead of time to prepare them for the activity but not so far in advance that they forget or lose the announcement.

To determine the most appropriate prompting system, the assessor might record the level of attendance following each type of prompt given the residents. To increase the likelihood that residents will attend activities, the following steps in prompting should be considered.

1. Written announcements should be posted throughout the facility, indicating the types of activities and the times and places they will be held.
2. If a loudspeaker or intercom system is available, announcements should be made an hour ahead of time, then 30 minutes before the activity, with a final call 10 to 15 minutes before the activity begins. This system will give residents time to get ready (grooming, going to the toilet, etc.). Residents who have hearing problems should be prompted by a staff member or other residents, following the same announcement schedule as the one recommended for the loudspeaker system. Jones, Brown, Noah, Jones, and Brezinski (1977) found that in an intermediate care facility resident prompters increased activity attendance by 100%.

    The director of activities should make sure that both resident and staff prompting takes place and should reinforce such prompting frequently. The director might keep an attendance roster with the names of various prompters beside the names of residents who usually need encouragement to attend activities. At the beginning of each session, the director can "call roll" and mention how important the prompters are in boosting attendance. In this way absences can be followed up to check on the reliability of prompters or the absent resident's ability to continue attending activities.

Attendance also may be increased by the type and arrangement of furniture in the activity area. Melin and Gotestam (1981) and Peterson, Knapp, Rosen, and Pither (1977) suggested small tables with chairs clustered around them to encourage social interaction among residents. However, the effect increased social interaction has on attendance rates has not been determined. The mental health practitioner should be careful to assess the effect of seating arrangements on residents in a particular facility. For example, if an arrangement increases the opportunity for people to socialize but the interaction itself is unpleasant, residents may regard attending the activity as aversive, even a type of "punishment."

In general, tables and chairs in the activity area should be placed away from doors where passing traffic may be distracting and away from air-conditioning units or other machinery. Noise and visual distractions may discourage people from attending the activities and even cause confusion in some residents. The chairs should provide firm support and be high enough so that residents can easily work with materials on top of the table. Avoid using hard chairs with wood or fiberglass backs and seats; they tend to become uncomfortable quickly.

Lighting is another factor to consider in assessing environmental conditions. Lighting should be adequate and evenly distributed throughout the activity area. However, make sure it is not too bright and that glare is minimized. Elderly residents with cataracts are especially affected by glare or bright light. The range of visual acuity is likely to vary within the population of any facility. As a result, at the beginning of an activity and throughout the program, encourage residents to report how well they can see various materials or activities involved.

The content of the activities and materials is also important. Selecting activities and materials on the basis of their reinforcement value has received little, if any, research attention. One cannot assume that any particular activity or material will or will not interest residents. Rather, one should assess the group being targeted for the activity program. Such an assessment would include the following:

1. An interview with each participant in a program activity to determine areas of interest as well as need.
2. For residents who may not be able to communicate their interests or needs, interviews with family members and friends and a study of the individual's social history.
3. Introducing a number of activities and materials at the same time to give residents a chance to choose among them.
4. Introducing activities and materials in a particular sequence and using a time-sampling technique to determine how long each resident spends on specific activities. A sample activity level form is included as Exhibit 3.1 at the end of this chapter.
5. Evaluating residents' capacities to determine whether they can do what is expected of them. For example, an intricate paint-by-number task should not be given to a resident who has hand tremors or visual acuity problems. In other cases, residents may be able to begin a task but find it too difficult or tiring to complete, and they abandon or avoid it.

The program director should assess these environmental variables before introducing an activity program and should continue to assess conditions throughout the program. The same variables should be considered for any resident who joins the program at a later date.

Assessing Resident Variables

The resident variables that need to be assessed, some of which we have touched on, include:

1. The physical ability of residents to get to the activity as scheduled.
2. Their ability to remember the time and place of the event.
3. Residents' capabilities to work with materials.
4. Psychological problems such as fear of being with a large group of people, of changes in routine, of becoming incontinent or lacking motor control, and of delusions associated with being in a group or with particular residents or staff (e.g., the possibility of being harmed by staff or other residents).

5. Behavior that might be disruptive and make the activity period less enjoyable and reinforcing for other residents.
6. Problems associated with medication that may prevent residents from attending or make attendance less reinforcing.

The director should consider two factors when assessing residents' ability to travel the distance from their rooms to the activity area. First, can residents get to the area without aid? Second, if so, is the effort residents must expend likely to discourage their continued attendance? Each resident's medical history can be checked for disorders that would hinder traveling to the activity area. Emphysema and other respiratory disorders or arthritis and other joint or bone problems would be conditions that might prevent residents from attempting the distance. Such information will also indicate problems residents may have in performing specific tasks or activities.

The assessor must be careful not to jump to conclusions about a resident's abilities when observing that nursing staff must help the person walk or move from place to place. Caretakers, as mentioned earlier, may reinforce dependent behavior in residents, doing for them what they would like to do independently.

The same caution should be exercised when asking residents whether they can get to an activity on their own. Residents may say no when actually they can travel the distance independently. One should not reinforce residents' reliance on others if they have the ability to walk or wheel themselves from one location to another. To check on residents' self-reports, observe them before and after meals to see whether they make it to and from the dining room by themselves and how difficult it is for them to do so. If residents are limited in their ability to walk or cannot get to the activities at all, another resident or staff member may be enlisted to help them. The assessor may want to keep a list pairing helpers with those who need assistance.

The second client variable to assess is residents' ability to remember the time and place of the activity. This capability can be assessed by using items from a geriatric assessment instrument that targets short-term memory function. Exhibit 3.2, following this chapter, provides a sample geriatric assessment form. Clients may be asked what they had for breakfast; the day, month, and year; or facts usually remembered easily such as who is the president of the United States or what is the name of the nursing home and town of residence. If short-term memory is severely impaired in a client, a resident or staff prompter can be used to remind the client of upcoming activities. With residents who have less severe memory problems, posting a written announcement in their rooms before each activity will remind them to attend.

The third client variable to consider is the residents' ability to engage in the activities that have been selected. The assessment is similar to that used for the ability to walk or ride to activities. Assessors should ask residents about their capabilities and check their medical histories for disorders that might restrict them, cause pain, limit motor control, and reduce visual and auditory discrimination. Cataracts, rheumatoid arthritis in the hands, Parkinson's disease, and other diseases or medication-related disorders can limit residents' abilities to engage in various types of activities.

In addition, the assessor should observe residents carefully while they are working to determine how difficult it is for them to manipulate materials. Does the resident drop items frequently? Hold materials close to the eyes? Does the client turn away from the activity often?

Once residents are assessed, materials and projects can be tailored to the limitations and strengths of each client. If someone has poor eyesight, the materials should be large and brightly colored and should not require fine visual discrimination. A resident who has problems with hand tremors should be given tasks requiring little fine motor control, instead using gross movements such as tossing rings. Also, residents can be grouped to complement each others' strengths. A client with poor eyesight but good motor control can be paired with someone who has good eyesight and poor motor control.

The fourth variable to consider is psychological problems that could make an activity unpleasant or punishing for the resident or for others. Again, the clinician should begin by studying the client's medical record for reports of fears of being embarrassed by incontinence or limited motor control, or of confusion, hallucinations, or delusions associated with cerebrovascular problems or Alzheimer's disease. Residents can be interviewed to determine problems that may not be mentioned in the medical record such as fears of crowding, thoughts of someone harming them if they attend the activity, or difficulty in adjusting to changes in routine. If a resident is reluctant to discuss such problems, the clinician could interview family members, roommates, friends, or facility personnel who may have gained the resident's confidence. In such interviews, the assessor should seek information regarding mental status (disorientation, hallucinations, delusions) and a history of particular behavior problems (phobias, general anxiety, difficulties getting along with others).

Residents who exhibit severely disorganized cognitive abilities probably will be difficult to keep on task in an activity. Without frequent prompting, they may wander away, stare into space, or bother other residents, which may provoke an aggressive response. We have had some success in keeping such residents on task by giving them simple, brightly colored puzzles to put together and by providing food as a primary reinforcement for completing the puzzle. Other methods include forming music groups where residents can hum along, clap, or participate at some level, and devising simple motor tasks such as throwing a ball to one another in a circle. Such activities can keep problem residents on task for short periods of time.

The initial approach with residents who are delusional or hallucinating should be medication. A low dose of one of the major tranquilizers can often help decrease the problem behaviors associated with psychosis. A resident who suffers from delusions or hallucinations and is angry or fearful as a result should not be involved in a group activity until such problems are brought under control.

Clients with fears of gatherings or changes in routine can sometimes be shaped slowly into attending the activity program. We have had some success with first bringing materials to the resident's living area while attempting to establish rapport with the client. We then introduce another resident into the living area to engage in the activity with the first client. The resident is asked to work with materials in the activity area at a time when a group is not using the room. As the resident becomes less fearful of working with another person and comes willingly to the activity area when a group is not present, the client is gradually introduced into group activities for a short time. Eventually, the resident begins to stay for a progressively longer period of time and to interact freely with others in the group.

CASE STUDY #1

A variant of such a shaping procedure was attempted with a 69-year-old female resident of a psychogeriatric ward. The client entered the cafeteria after other residents and ate by herself. At the token store she waited to be the last in line, keeping about 5 to 6 feet between herself and others. All attempts to engage her in conversation were met with curt "yes" or "no" responses and at times with hostility. On occasion, repeated physical or verbal prompts to attend activities or therapy resulted in aggressive reactions on her part. Her chart indicated a history of delusions and hallucinations. She had been diagnosed during previous hospitalizations as paranoid schizophrenic.

A shaping treatment was initiated. At first, a staff member would drop off material at the client's room and pick it up again at the end of every activity period. After a time, the staff member began staying for increasing lengths of time to show the client how to use the materials. The resident was thanked for letting the staff member stay, and was given bonus points on her token card. The resident began to talk more with the staff member during these sessions.

After several weeks, a chair was placed in the hall next to the group activity area. The resident was told that to continue receiving bonus points, she would have to sit in the hall chair. The staff member began placing activity materials on the chair. When the resident sat in the chair, the staff member would spend time with her and give her bonus points at the end of the activity.

This procedure continued until the resident managed to sit through the activity period at a table in the lobby activity area. She was awarded points for entering the area and remaining half-way through the period, with bonus points given if she stayed until the end. At first she remained only for a brief time, particularly if another resident sat at her table. However, in a matter of weeks, she was attending most activity periods and remaining through to the end. She was also engaging in increased levels of conversation with other residents.

The fifth resident variable to consider is behavior that might be disruptive, making the activity period less reinforcing for other residents. We have already briefly mentioned two such problems. One is the confused, disoriented client who frequently wanders about the activity area, grabs or clings to other residents, or picks up materials from tables. The other is the psychotic resident who suffers from delusions and hallucinations and as a result may be hostile or fearful around others. (See also Chapter 4 for techniques on dealing with behavioral excesses.)

The sixth variable involves problems associated with medication when they prevent residents from participating in activities or make their participation less reinforcing. For example, tranquilizers often induce drowsiness, which interferes with a client's concentration and may increase the effort it takes to attend activities. Residents who often fall asleep during activities, yawn, or exhibit other behaviors associated with drowsiness may be experiencing side-effects of their medication. Other drugs may cause psychotic-like behavior or restlessness, problems that can be remedied by asking the physician to reduce or discontinue the medication or to add a medication to diminish these side-effects. (See Chapter 6 for a more detailed description of medications and their adverse effects.)

Increasing Residents' Ambulation

A major problem in increasing residents' activity levels concerns clients who refuse to walk or roll a wheelchair even though they have no medical problems or physical limitations that would prevent them from doing so. The resulting inactivity can have serious consequences for clients' general mental and physical health.

A study by Bonner (1969) has outlined some of the problems associated with sitting or lying down for long periods without exercising. Patients are likely to experience improper elimination, less efficient functioning of the respiratory system, muscle atrophy, a higher risk of vasomotor instability, labile blood pressure, and decreases in bone mass.

As a result, various behavioral techniques have been designed to increase ambulation in an elderly population. Mac-Donald and Butler (1974) increased walking in two elderly residents of a nursing home who had been in wheelchairs for several months, although neither had any medical problem that prevented them from walking. The authors simply prompted the residents by asking them to walk to the dining room and by offering to help them get out of their wheelchairs. When the residents did so, they were praised and given social interaction. When they did not, the reinforcers were withheld. During phase one of the study, the residents walked to their assigned seats in the dining room for 10 consecutive days. During the reversal phase, the rate fell to zero. When the contingencies were reinstated, the residents again walked to their seats for 15 out of 16 days.

Sachs (1975) conducted two case studies in which behavioral techniques were used to increase walking behavior. In one case, an 88-year-old woman who spent little time out of her wheelchair or room was given points for every minute she walked. The points could be exchanged for back-up reinforcers. Her mobility was significantly increased, and she spent less time by herself. In the second case, a 64-year-old man with Parkinson's disease was given tokens for each 25 feet traveled with or without the aid of wooden side rails. He was told that his progress was being timed. During treatment, the client increased the distance he covered and shortened the time it took him to begin walking. We have found in our experience on a psychogeriatric unit that such differential reinforcement of walking is enough to significantly increase the behavior.

In assessing ambulation problems, two factors are critical. First, one must identify and control the resident's "helpers," those staff members and clients who will help the resident when assistance is not actually needed. Second, one should make sure that no medical problems exist that should be treated before starting an ambulation program. Often the elderly client who refuses to walk will use somatic complaints as an excuse. When such complaints are followed up by a physician, usually no physiological basis is found. As a result, staff members may come to believe that all such complaints are excuses and fail to check for medical problems. They may believe the client can walk when in fact there is some genuine physical disorder. The clinician should always have medical personnel conduct a thorough assessment of such complaints before attempting a behavioral intervention and should monitor the client throughout the program.

One approach for increasing ambulation involves the following steps:

1. Make sure the client is not helped to walk unless it is absolutely necessary. If a client has a special diet prescribed or at times has refused to eat, assign a staff member to accompany the resident to the dining area. Otherwise, offer no assistance in walking. If the client has to be helped to meals, social interaction with the individual should not take place.
2. If the client has not walked for some time, a shaping process may be used to encourage walking short distances.

Reinforcers might include social interaction, praise, food, or other forms of age-appropriate rewards contingent upon the client's response. The distance could be slowly increased according to the client's abilities. If the person has problems standing or walking at first, a period of physical therapy may be necessary before instituting a behavioral program to increase ambulation.

3. The client should be prompted frequently by staff to walk and offered social reinforcement for doing so. However, staff members should also notice when the client is tiring and stop the session. Otherwise, the reinforcing effects of walking could be diminished.

Some elderly clients will refuse to give up their wheelchair or walker because they are afraid of falling. If the client's history indicates that intermittent falling is a problem, then it may be appropriate for the client to walk with aid. On the other hand, if the wheelchair or walker is clearly not needed and the client is still afraid of being without it, then an intervention designed to fade its use slowly may be the best approach. Such an intervention could involve the following steps conducted in several sessions during the day.

1. Walking while holding the arm of a staff member.
2. Walking holding only the hand of the staff member.
3. Walking beside the staff member with the client's hand held out toward the caretaker but not touching.
4. Gradually increasing the time the client walks beside the staff member without touching and slowly widening the distance between the staff member and client.

Elderly people are usually more cautious about walking than their younger counterparts, and often for good reason since many of them experience problems with balance. As a result, the clinician and other staff members involved should understand that they must fade the supports slowly and stay well within the boundaries of what the client can tolerate without provoking undue anxiety. Generous praise should be given for any increase the client makes in independent ambulation.

CASE STUDY #2

A 74-year-old female resident of a geropsychiatric facility had fallen and fractured her hip. She had spent several months in a wheelchair during her recuperation. With physical therapy, she regained the ability to move about with a walker and could have progressed to independent walking. However, she refused to give up the walker and expressed a fear of falling if she attempted to walk unaided. Her meals were brought to her on the ward, but members of the treatment team considered this practice as probably reinforcing her refusal to walk independently.

A program was initiated whereby she was prompted to walk holding onto a staff member's arm during a 30-minute session in the morning and another session in the evening. This activity was reinforced by staff through praise and attention. At other times she was transported by wheelchair during which a minimum of staff attention was paid to her. These sessions continued for several weeks until she appeared to show little or no anxiety about walking with staff members.

During the second phase of the intervention, the staff member took her to a point about 3 to 4 feet from a chair. She was instructed to let go of the staff member's arm and walk unaided to the chair. She was reassured continually that the staff member would not let her fall, would help her into the chair, and would be within reach if she wanted to grasp his arm. The staff member walked closely beside her, and she occasionally took his arm, although never more than twice in a session and then only for brief moments. She was generously praised for walking unaided. The length of these sessions varied, depending on how long it took her to walk to the chair.

The next step was to place a piece of tape on the floor at the point where the client started walking and extend it to the chair. Once she could walk without support along the tape for 4 days (eight sessions), the tape was moved 2 or 3 feet farther from the chair.

Each time she met a 4-day criteria, her progress was praised generously by all of the staff members who were working with her. This phase of the intervention was continued until she could walk unsupported from her bed to the chair in the lobby, a distance of about 50 to 60 feet. During these sessions, the staff member followed her less closely.

The client was finally able to walk independently from almost any point on the ward. She began spontaneously walking to the dining room and back on her own. She continued to have some apprehension about walking unaided in a group or when numerous residents were milling about the ward. However, she was discharged from the hospital before an intervention could be developed to target this concern.

Treating Urinary Incontinence

Urinary and fecal incontinence is often a significant problem within a geriatric population. One study estimates that 85% of the incontinence observed in a hospital setting occurs in people 65 years of age or older (Lowenthal, 1958).

Such problems are often associated with age-related changes such as diminished bladder capacity, a lessening of urinary efficiency where some residual urine may remain after urination, involuntary contraction of the bladder, slow ambulation, and loss of the ability to sense the need to void. Changes due to cerebral deterioration, cardiovascular problems, infection, and toxic effects of medication may also produce periods of confusion and disorientation during which the elderly person is unable to locate the toilet.

Several investigators have used behavioral principles to decrease incontinence within an elderly population. Blackman (1977) decreased the average daily rate of urinary incontinence by 60% among 15 female residents of a nursing facility. Techniques used included positive reinforcement of appropriate urination and retention, and scheduling toilet trips to enhance stimulus control (immediately after rising in the morning and after meals).

Sanavio (1981) modified techniques used by Foxx and Azrin (1973) to decrease urinary incontinence in a 60-year-old client and fecal incontinence in a 77-year-old client. Both were residents of a psychiatric facility. By using positive reinforcement of appropriate voiding and retention and a combination of correction and positive practice for accidents detected by use of a wet-alert buzzer, he reduced incontinence for both clients to zero incidents during the treatment phase.

Atthowe (1972) used techniques of punishment and negative and positive reinforcement to decrease nocturnal incontinence in 12 patients hospitalized over 20 years. The punishment techniques consisted of night awakenings and toilet trips combined with residence in less pleasing sleeping quarters. Negative reinforcement techniques included fading of nightly bathroom trips and a chance to move to more desirable sleeping quarters provided continence was maintained. Positive reinforcement consisted of morning tokens for remaining dry throughout the night.

Assessment

The intervention used should be the result of assessing each link in the chain of behaviors necessary for appropriate toileting. These links include:

1. Awareness of the urge to urinate.
2. Ability to locate and get to the toilet.
3. Ability to undress and dress and perform other necessary behaviors in the toileting sequence.

Assessing toileting ability should involve the following steps:

1. An interview with medical personnel to determine if a physiological problem exists that must be treated before beginning a toileting program. Such conditions as urinary tract infections, prostate disorder, uncontrolled diabetes, muscle atrophy, or confusion and disorientation resulting from illness or medication can render any toileting program useless. It is important for the clinician to make sure that intervention has the best chance of succeeding.
2. An interview with the client to determine the client's mental state, ability to request toileting, awareness of bladder distention, and overall ability and motivation to comply with the intervention.
3. Observation of the client during toileting or gathering information from a staff member or others who have observed the client. Such information will tell the clinician whether the client can locate and get to the toilet, negotiate barriers, and complete the toileting sequence (undressing, sitting or standing before the toilet, wiping, flushing, and the like).
4. Establishing a baseline of toileting accidents (when, where, how often).

If clients cannot remember experiencing bladder distention, they may be offered fluids several times over a 4- to 6-hour period and asked frequently if they need to use the toilet. In addition, during this time, clients should be taken to the toilet on the hour to decrease chances of an accident. If clients do not report any urge to urinate, they are not likely to be aware of bladder distention. If the urge to urinate is present but only when near the toilet, some form of stimulus control training may be required (see Chapter 5).

A baseline of toileting behavior may be obtained by staff recording the frequency and times of appropriate voiding and accidents over 2 or 3 days. Checks should be made each hour. Exhibit 3.3 at the end of this chapter provides a sample urinary incontinence recording form. Questions to be answered by using such a baseline include:

1. How long can a client go between toileting trips before an accident occurs (an index of bladder control)?
2. When do more accidents occur (at night, when a particular staff member is conducting toilet training, etc.)?
3. How many accidents actually occurred prior to intervention (a baseline)?

Treatment

The assessment should result in one or more treatments designed to correct the client's particular deficits in the toileting behavior chain. For example, if the client has little or no awareness of bladder distention, reinforcing client requests to go to the toilet is not likely to correct the problem. Some biofeedback techniques can be used to increase such awareness (Burgio, Whitehead, Engel, & Middaugh, 1984). However, a more practical approach might be to reduce reliance on client requests and instead use some external time-related stimulus such as an hourly alarm on a watch, clock, or kitchen timer as a cue to go to the toilet.

If clients cannot get to the toilet independently, the clinician may consider several options. They may be able to use a portable toilet, provided they can lift themselves onto the seat. If this is not possible, use of a hand-held urinal or bedpan may be another alternative. In introducing any of these options, the clinician must be careful to enlist the clients' support and to assess the response cost involved in lifting themselves from the bed to the toilet and back. Also, some people find using urinals and bedpans aesthetically unacceptable.

Some clients may be able to get to the toilet on their own but are too disoriented to locate it. In such cases, interventions involving stimulus control may be needed (see Chapter 5 for detailed descriptions of such techniques).

Some clients are aware of the need to urinate but may be unable to undress or dress themselves or complete the full chain of behaviors in the toileting sequence. Reinforcing requests for assistance is one way to handle this problem, as suggested by Schnelle, Traughber, Morgan, Embry, Binion, and Coleman (1983). Such an intervention involves first telling the client that such assistance is available and how to request it. The client should then be offered help according to the toileting schedule established for the individual, and the acceptance of offers reinforced. Spontaneous requests for assistance should be answered promptly and socially reinforced.

The following steps in toilet training, similar to those outlined by Hussian (1981), may be implemented with adjustments as needed for individual differences. The approach combines stimulus control, feedback, and contingent positive reinforcement.

1. Take the client to the toilet within 15 minutes of awakening.
2. If voiding does not occur, prompt the resident to go to the toilet every half hour.
3. If voiding does occur, prompt the resident to toilet every hour after that time and reinforce for compliance.
4. Reinforce the resident for voiding appropriately.
5. After 4 hours of no voiding, toilet every half hour.
6. Prompt the resident to go to the toilet within 15 to 20 minutes following an accident.

Increasing Self-Care Skills

Behavioral interventions targeting grooming and eating skills can help residents remain more self-sufficient and relieve staff of many time-consuming tasks.

Increasing Self-Grooming Skills

Behavioral techniques frequently have been used to correct deficits in a mentally retarded population (Girardeau & Spradlin, 1964; Hunt, Fitzhugh, & Fitzhugh, 1968). However, only a few studies have been done on applying the approach to elderly clients. In one report, Rinke, Williams, and Lloyd (1978) cited some success in increasing self-bathing in six nursing home residents. The intervention combined physical prompts (manual guidance) with verbal prompts (instructions) for several behavior categories involved in self-bathing (undressing, soaping, rinsing, drying, and dressing). The authors found that a combination of prompting and reinforcement (choice of types of food or grooming aids after each session) increased self-care in each behavior category.

Sachs (1975) used behavioral techniques to increase oral hygiene in three elderly residents of a nursing home. The first step of the treatment involved using tokens to reinforce residents when they brushed their teeth within 30 minutes after each meal. In step two, tokens were used to reinforce clients for picking up their toothbrushes from the nursing station, brushing their teeth, and returning the toothbrushes within 30 minutes after completing the task. Two residents responded by brushing their teeth more often. However, the rate of brushing for one resident fell when the treatment required picking up and returning the toothbrush.

Assessment. Elderly clients may stop grooming themselves for several reasons. In some facilities staff may do the grooming for them, or they may have physical problems such as arthritis or tremors that make performing such tasks difficult and painful. In other cases, memory impairment may be severe enough that clients simply forget the need to groom. The clinician should keep these factors in mind when assessing clients' conditions.

Treatment. If the nursing staff have taken over most or all of the clients' self-grooming tasks, treatment may consist of instructing the staff to allow residents to remain as independent as possible. Frequently, the staff will complain that letting residents groom themselves requires too much time. In such cases, the clinician may need to review daily schedules with supervisory personnel to allow residents enough time to complete grooming on their own.

If clients have stopped grooming because of physical limitations, it may not be possible for them to be fully independent in this task again. However, residents may be able to do parts of the task or use modified grooming aids that make self-grooming easier. For example, the handles of brushes or toothbrushes can be built up with foam rubber and tape so that residents suffering from arthritis or tremors can hold them more comfortably.

Clients with severe memory problems may forget that grooming is necessary. They may also believe they have just finished bathing, brushing their teeth, or combing their hair when in fact they did so several hours or days ago. Some of these clients may simply need to be reminded to complete grooming tasks.

With other clients, memory problems may be too severe for verbal prompts to work. They may forget the reminder seconds after it is given. In such cases, stimulus control techniques may be used. This approach could involve taking the client to the grooming area at the same time each day and making sure that the area and grooming aids used are changed as little as possible. The same prompts may be used at each grooming session, for example, placing the resident in front of a mirror, rubbing one's hand across his beard while holding a razor or electric shaver before the client's eyes, and using the verbal prompt "shave."

A combination of prompts that engages several of the clients' senses can strengthen the effectiveness of the stimuli. This approach can be especially helpful when the client's attention wanders and the grooming stops. A verbal prompt to continue can be given, along with a social or primary reinforcer when the client does so. If grooming does not resume with a verbal prompt, it should be paired with a physical prompt. For example, say the word "shave" and gently guide the resident's hand holding the razor back to his face, simultaneously prompting him to look at himself in the mirror if his gaze wanders.

Generally, the grooming experience should be made as pleasant as possible for the client. Use social and primary reinforcers such as food or drink when the client has entered the grooming area, and use them again when each link in the grooming chain is completed.

Below are the steps to be followed in the grooming training sequence:

1. Separate the chain of grooming behaviors into individual links or steps. Table 3.1 provides an example of such a behavioral chain for shaving.
2. When training clients in grooming skills, maximize stimulus control by grooming in the same area. Make sure that instruments, prompts, and steps in the task are varied as little as possible.
3. Train clients one step at a time. One can begin with the first link in the behavioral chain—or at the start of the task—and train clients in each successive link (forward chaining); or one can begin with the last link and move toward the first (backward chaining).
4. Allow clients to do as much as possible without prompting. If prompts are needed, begin first with a verbal prompt and

TABLE 3.1
A BEHAVIORAL CHAIN FOR SHAVING

1. Walks from door of grooming area to sink.
2. Stands before sink and makes eye contact with image in mirror.
3. Turns on water.
4. Cups water in hands and splashes on face.
5. Picks up can of shaving cream and squirts appropriate amount in palm of hand.
6. Places shaving cream on beard.
7. Picks up razor.
8. Shaves sideburn/jaw area of right side of face.
9. Shaves sideburn/jaw area of left side of face.
10. Shaves chin area.
11. Shaves underneath chin and neck area.
12. Rinses razor.
13. Rinses and dries face.

reinforce the clients immediately when the prompt is followed. If physical prompting is necessary, begin with a verbal prompt and wait several seconds. Should clients fail to
comply, give another verbal prompt and immediately guide
them manually through the behavior, giving only the guidance that is necessary.

5. Withdraw guidance when the client begins to respond
independently, and reinforce the response. Even if manual
guidance is necessary at some point in the chain, reinforce the client at the end of the response. After reinforcing
the manually guided response several times, attempt to
fade such prompts. Begin as close as possible to the
moment when manual guidance was needed and try a verbal prompt alone.

The elderly demented client is not likely to achieve complete
independence in grooming. However, training can help such
clients be as self-sufficient as possible given their physical and
cognitive limitations.

Increasing Independent Eating Skills

Eating skills are another major area of self-care in which behavioral interventions may prove effective. For example, Geiger and
Johnson (1974) increased correct eating behavior of six elderly residents by contracting for positive reinforcement to be delivered
after meals in which residents displayed appropriate behavior.

In another case study by Baltes and Zerbe (1976a), the
authors found that clients' correct eating behaviors increased

after a combination of techniques had been used. The authors modified eating utensils to make them easier to hold and provided social reinforcement when clients used the utensils independently. A second study by Baltes and Zerbe (1976b) reported their attempts to help a 67-year-old nursing home resident regain the ability to feed himself. The authors used a combination of verbal prompting and immediate reinforcement whenever the resident fed himself successfully. They also employed a time-out procedure for undesirable behavior. For example, if the client dumped his food on the floor, reinforcers were removed and the experimenter turned away from the subject. Baltes and Zerbe were successful in increasing independent eating responses from only 0 to 3 responses to a range of 4 to 25 responses during treatment.

Assessment. Clinicians should make sure that clients are checked for physical disorders or problems that may prevent them from feeding themselves. It may be their inability to eat independently is caused by arthritis, hand tremors, visual problems, side-effects of medication, or psychological factors.

Clinicians and staff should conduct a functional analysis of the behavior to determine exactly what types of inappropriate behavior take place, in what setting, and how often they occur.

Treatment. Training the elderly in eating skills is similar to the methods used to increase independent grooming. The clinician should first make sure that all physical limitations and problems are treated before any program is initiated. As in training clients to groom themselves, stimulus control is most effective when the client eats in the same place every day with little variation in utensils and routine. Modifying utensils, such as building up handles with foam rubber and tape, can make it easier for clients with arthritis and other manual dexterity problems to use knives, forks, and spoons. Cups with large handles may also be used for the same purpose.

For clients with visual acuity problems, the color of dishes should contrast with the tablecloth so they can be seen clearly. Glass plates or cups should not be used; they are not only more difficult to discriminate from the background, but also they can be broken easily.

The effort involved in eating can be reduced by cutting up meats and altering the consistency and appearance of food to accommodate the clients' fine motor skills and ability to chew. Residents might also wear a plastic covering over clothes to minimize soiling and the discomfort of dropping food and drink on themselves.

As in the case of grooming skills, the eating process can be separated into a series of steps, although the steps are likely to be more repetitious. Backward chaining is probably the best training technique since there is a natural reinforcer at the end of the behavior chain—namely, putting food or drink in the mouth. The suggestions regarding verbal prompting and manual guidance used in grooming are appropriate for training in eating skills.

Other techniques have proved useful in increasing correct eating behavior and decreasing inappropriate responses. We found that using a brief time out helped decrease undesirable eating behavior (eating too fast, dropping utensils and eating with hands, food dumping). Simply push the client's tray out of reach and provide no attention for the person for 15 to 30 seconds.

Differential reinforcement of other behavior (DRO) is another technique that often works well. In this approach, a favorite food or drink is given at intervals throughout the meal for *not* engaging in any inappropriate mealtime behavior. The DRO reinforcement interval is set by how long a client refrains from engaging in inappropriate behavior during a meal. Such information should be gathered before a program is started. If the client can eat for 10 minutes without dumping food on the floor, the DRO interval would be set at 8 to 9 minutes. This step ensures that reinforcement takes place for the *absence* of inappropriate responses.

Other eating problems that may arise include clients' refusal to eat or their desire to eat only certain foods. Any complaint about loss of appetite should be followed up to determine if a physiological problem exists. Loss of appetite may also indicate depression. The clinician may need to treat that disorder rather than attend to the eating problem.

We have found that the Premack Principle can be used occasionally as an intervention when clients refuse to eat. With this approach, clients are allowed to engage in a favorite activity or have a session with a favorite staff member only after eating a portion of the meal. Another similar intervention involves giving clients tokens for bites of food swallowed. The tokens can be traded in after the meal for cigarettes, coffee, or other preferred items.

For clients who exhibit a severely limited food preference, we have had some success with making favorite foods a reinforcer for eating less preferred items. One elderly client liked ice cream and various desserts better than other types of food and would eat little else if left to himself. He was given a spoonful of ice cream after each three bites of a less preferred food, a technique that significantly altered his eating behavior toward consuming a more balanced diet.

Increasing Social Interactions

In many cases, social interactions in an elderly population may decrease because of the death or loss of friends and family, physical limitations, and increased hesitancy to make new social contacts. As a result, the level of social interaction among elderly residents should be an important target for clinical intervention. Some studies indicate that intimate contacts lead to increased satisfaction in an elderly population (Jeffers & Nichols, 1961) and help prevent the possible negative effects of isolation (Ernst, Beran, Safford, & Kleinhauz, 1978).

Various interventions have been used to increase social interactions among the elderly. Some investigators (Blackman, Howe, & Pinkston, 1976; Quilitch, 1974) have found that offering regularly planned activities can significantly increase social contacts. Other researchers (Peterson, Knapp, Rosen, & Pither, 1977) noted that rearranging furniture to encourage conversation (for example, putting chairs around tables) increased the level of verbal interaction among elderly residents.

Mueller and Atlas (1972) used tokens and primary reinforcers to raise the level of verbal communication of five elderly residents. Nigl and Jackson (1981) significantly increased appropriate communication among residents by using tokens that could be exchanged for food, cigarettes, and other items. They found that such behavioral interventions considerably increased the rate of social behavior. O'Quin and O'Dell (1981) raised the level of staff/resident interaction with a combination of training, instructions, social approval, and feedback.

Hoyer, Kafer, Simpson, and Hoyer (1974) used pennies to reinforce conversation among four elderly residents who rarely spoke to staff or other clients. When the investigators alternated reinforcement and extinction intervals, they found that verbal communication increased during reinforcement intervals. In addition, two of the residents increased the number of words they spoke that were not directly reinforced. The investigators attributed this response to the possible effects of modeling.

Verbal interactions among four elderly retarded males were increased by Kleitsch, Whitman, and Santos (1983). The authors employed a training procedure that combined verbal prompts, modeling, and behavioral rehearsal. Social praise and conversation were employed to reinforce social interaction designed for use with a variety of clients and a range of conversational topics. The technique helped to promote generalization of the behavior.

Assessment.

When implementing a social interaction program, the clinician should start by identifying those residents who seldom speak with others. This information can be recorded as part of the activity level of each resident (see Exhibit 3.1 at the end of this chapter). Residents can be observed at particular times during the day and their behavior recorded within a specific class of behaviors (conversing with another resident, manipulating materials, working at or completing a task, and the like) for a 15-minute period. The intervals in which residents are observed relating with others can be added up and divided by the total number of intervals in order to obtain the rate of interaction for each resident.

The second step in the process is to explore reasons for low social interaction levels. The clinician should pinpoint conditions that might limit a client's ability to interact or that might decrease the chances of an intervention succeeding. Some of the causes contributing to low social interaction include:

1. Severe memory or language problems that seriously impair social exchange.
2. Side-effects of medication (such as drowsiness) that limit a resident's ability to pay attention to an ongoing conversation.
3. Delusions on the resident's part that some harm will result from engaging in conversation or other types of social interaction.
4. The resident's belief that proper introductions should precede interaction with others.
5. Not knowing what to talk about with others.
6. The resident's interpersonal anxiety that prevents either initiating or maintaining a conversation.
7. Deep depression that results in a desire to be left alone.
8. Hearing deficits that make conversation unintelligible and therefore something to be avoided.

Many of these and other contributing causes can be assessed by interviewing clients using the geriatric assessment Form (see Exhibit 3.2). This instrument allows the clinician to evaluate memory function, indicators of depression, and the presence of hallucinations and delusions.

If residents exhibit such severe memory problems that they cannot carry on meaningful conversations, a social interaction program is not likely to be effective. In such cases, it may be best to involve residents in a music or movement group where verbal communication is not required. However, the clinician should never assume from the interview that disorganized verbal skills are the result solely of a chronic progressive dementia. The resident's medical history and family and friends should be consulted to determine if the client's behavioral picture can be associated with some type of acute condition (see Chapter 6).

If the client is continually lethargic or drowsy, suspect the side-effects of some medication the resident may be taking. This condition would require some adjustment in the drug's dosage or in the number of times it is taken. After the client's drug intake has been modified, conduct a second assessment to determine if the resident continues to show a low level of social interaction.

Residents who are hallucinating or suffering from delusions should be checked to see if the condition is chronic or the result of some acute physiological disorder. Information about time of onset, chronicity, and environmental stressors may help answer this question. If the condition is chronic, an adjustment in the medication level may help control the problem. We have found that psychotropic medications will not always eliminate delusions, although the emotional upset associated with them may be reduced somewhat. In that case, behavioral interventions together with medication may be effective in increasing social interactions clients previously avoided because of delusions.

Treatment.

Residents with such problems should be shaped into engaging in interpersonal contact and conversation. The clinician or staff member should first meet individually with the resident, engaging only in as much conversation as the client can tolerate. If the resident begins to talk more often about the delusions, it is best to reduce contact with the person. However, be sure the program is not so demanding that it precipitates the very behavior the clinician is seeking to reduce.

Individual contacts with the client should continue until the resident feels comfortable in conversing with one person. At that point, a second person may be brought in. The second person at first may sit quietly and not join the conversation unless requested by the target resident. Avoid discussing delusional material with the client since this may upset the person or positively reinforce the behavior. If the resident begins to talk about delusions, the clinician should either direct the resident to another topic or turn away and not enter into the conversation until the behavior stops. Other residents should never be left alone with the client unless the clinician can be sure they will not inadvertently reinforce the delusional behavior.

At some point early in the intervention, the clinician should suggest to the resident that the two of them visit an activity area or other place where group interaction is likely to occur. This step will enable the client to get used to a new environment before group members are introduced. At first, make sure only those people with whom the resident has conversed in the living area are present in the environment. Later, others may be introduced.

A social interaction program may be appropriate in some cases for a depressed resident. However, the clinician should also consider additional interventions such as antidepressant medication and strategies to change depressive thought patterns. Often tangible reinforcers can encourage a resident to attend group meetings and activities and to interact socially.

Hearing-impaired residents may benefit more from one-to-one interaction, particularly in a place where background noise is low, than from group activities. In our experience, residents with hearing problems do rather poorly in group interaction since they cannot follow the conversation. As a result, they either do not participate or they make comments that have little to do with the topic of conversation. If the hearing-impaired resident does take part in a group conversation, background noise and other conversations must be minimized and participants prompted to speak slowly and distinctly. Unfortunately, elderly people often speak more softly and stammer or repeat words more frequently than do younger people, which may compound the problem.

Social interaction of hearing-impaired clients might be increased by introducing a project that two people can work on. The project should require conversation and may be completed in the residents' living area where background noise is less. The clinician could enter into a contingency contract with the two participants that would provide some form of reinforcement when they have completed a portion of the project. (Appendix A provides a sample contingency contract.)

Some residents experience considerable anxiety when they must speak with others. They do not know how to initiate a conversation or how to maintain it. The following recommendations may be helpful in conducting a social interaction group.

The clinician should meet with these residents individually until their anxiety is reduced while talking with one person. The clinician can help this process by making little or no demand for a particular rate of conversation and also by introducing relaxation exercises (Goldfried & Davidson, 1976). At some point in these meetings, the clinician and resident might discuss what aspects of conversation cause anxiety (opening a conversation, maintaining it, answering questions).

The clinician might help the client roleplay those behaviors that produce the most anxiety. At first, the clinician may model appropriate conversational skills and, when necessary, coach the resident in developing and using such skills. During this process, the clinician should make liberal use of praise and positive feedback to help reduce the client's anxiety. When the resident can converse easily with the clinician and reports that the anxiety is well within the tolerance range, the resident should be asked to attend a group.

Within the group setting, the client should not be pressured to engage in conversation either by the clinician or by other participants. If after several sessions the resident has not entered into group conversation, the clinician may want to contract with the client to engage in the least threatening social behavior (e.g., answering questions, initiating a conversation, asking questions). The clinician should then reinforce the resident by praising any conversational skill the person uses within the group.

The social interaction group may differ according to the needs of each resident. If conversational skills and anxiety are the predominant problems, then the clinician may rehearse appropriate skills with the client, using modeling and instruction. If the major problem is depression, then the group might talk about subjects that invoke a lighter mood (e.g., pleasant or rewarding past experiences). The clinician might also contract with individuals in the group to engage in tasks that are potentially reinforcing to the depressed client to increase the appropriate response rate. With an elderly population, such groups in general should be directive but not confrontive or intimidating to clients. The leader should be tolerant of some residents' slower progress and their greater caution in social interactions.

EXHIBIT 3.1
ACTIVITY LEVEL FORM

Client

Date

Ward

Observer 1

Observer 2

Activity Time begun:	Observation time													
	1	2	3	4	5	6	7	8	9	10	11	12	13	14
Talking with 1 client														
Talking with 2+ clients														
Talking with 1 staff member														
Talking with 2+ staff members														
Solitary game, non-prompted														
Solitary game, prompted														
Game with others, non-prompted														
Game with others, prompted														
Reading														
Watching television														
Ambulating														
Exercise														
Sitting on floor														
In bathroom or restroom														
Self-stimulation _____														
Eating														
Smoking														
Manipulating object _____														
Off-ward activity														
On bed, awake														
On bed, asleep														
On chair, awake														
On chair, asleep														
Verbal abuse														
Physical aggression														
In time out														
In seclusion														
Other (please specify) _____														
_____														
_____														
_____														

Additional comments _____

EXHIBIT 3.2
GERIATRIC ASSESSMENT FORM

Client _____   Date & time _____

Date of birth _____   Interviewer _____

Ward _____

Check (✓) incorrect responses.
1. What is the name of this place? _____
2. What is today's date? _____
3. What month is it? _____
4. What is the year? _____
5. How old are you? _____
6. When is your birthday? _____
7. Where were you born? _____
8. Who is the president of the United States? _____
9. Who was the president before him? _____

I am going to give you three words which I would like for you to repeat now and when I ask again in three minutes. These words are: chair, door, tree.

1. _____   2. _____

EXHIBIT 3.3
URINARY INCONTINENCE RECORDING FORM

Client _____

Room and bed no. _____

Date _____

Staff _____

Hours since awakening

Date	Assisted to toilet in AM (✓)	V (✓)	1		2		3		4		5		6		7		8		9		10		11		12		13		14		15		16		17		18	
				½		½		½		½		½		½		½		½		½		½		½		½		½		½		½		½		½		½

Codes: O = Offered toileting   A = Accepted   NA = Not accepted   V = Voided   NV = No voiding   W = Wet   D = Dry

4
Assessment and Treatment of Behavioral Excesses

Even though elderly clients often exhibit *excessive* behaviors, their behavioral *deficits* have long been the major focus of behavioral assessment and intervention in geriatrics (Hussian, 1984). The emphasis on identifying and treating deficits may be the result of several factors.

1. Traditionally, aging is associated with loss or debility and not with increases in behavior. Though far from an accurate description of the normal aging process, this model has fostered methods to re-establish responses that have declined with age. In fact, most of the observations made during the early phases of geriatrics focused almost exclusively on residents' lack of movement or responsiveness to their surroundings. Such observations may be accurate to some extent within institutions. However, *excessive* behaviors, not deficits, are more responsible for residents suffering such consequences as restriction, seclusion, medication, segregation, or avoidance within institutional settings.

2. Interventions to increase responses are regarded as more "positive" and less invasive than response reduction techniques. In general, interventions designed to increase a client's response rate are viewed as less demeaning, unless the activities or stimuli provided are too "childish" for the client's age and abilities. These techniques also involve far less oversight by treatment review parties. At times, however, efforts to protect individuals from "undesirable"

treatment fail to safeguard the rights of others and may even prevent patients from receiving appropriate treatment for their excessive behaviors.

As a result, many interventions for behavioral excesses involve lengthy procedures to obtain permission for their use. Such questions as a client's competency, right to refuse treatment, right to have basic necessities, and status on admission may be difficult to answer with any certainty. In the meantime, the client's excessive behavior continues.

3. Initial reports emphasized behavioral techniques applied to deficit problems of elderly clients. Thus, the trend was set from the beginning to use behavioral methods such as prompting and reinforcement to increase low response rates (e.g., low level of participation in activities, walking independently, etc.). Subsequent work continued this trend since little independent analysis was conducted of other types of responses. Although these early studies yielded important information, investigators over the years have tended to focus on behavioral deficits to the exclusion of other responses.

Assessing and Treating Excessive Behaviors

Currently, excessive behaviors in the elderly are receiving more attention. *Behavioral excesses* are defined as those responses that occur at higher than acceptable rates. Such responses include shouting, cursing, physical aggression, stripping, chronic complaints or demands, and shadowing (following others closely). Investigators and mental health professionals now recognize such behaviors as valid targets for change for the following reasons (Hussian, 1984).

1. Some of these responses can be dangerous to the client and others and may damage property.
2. Such behaviors can disrupt or diminish the benefits of programs designed for the client or for others in the same locale.
3. These responses often result in consequences that remove the client from constructive activities or therapies. The time the client spends in seclusion, time out, restriction, segregation, or under medication may be longer than the time spent engaging in the target behavior. This situation reduces the client's ability to interact with others.

4. Staff may also spend more time dealing with the client's excessive behavior, or the results of such behavior, than in more constructive pursuits. Attempts to provide social reinforcement, shaping, prompting, and teaching must be suspended while the staff tries to control or modify the client's excessive responses.

5. Visitors and staff may avoid clients who exhibit excessive behavior or may not include them when designing programs. Such social isolation prevents the client from receiving necessary feedback from staff and other residents.

6. Excessive behavior of clients can damage staff morale and increase the turnover rate in a facility. Some staff may even be injured. Certainly, all staff members will experience higher levels of stress.

7. Certain excessive behavior (yelling, aggression, chronic complaints or demands) will severely limit a client's placement alternatives. Not many facilities are willing to accept clients known for their excessive behavior.

Inappropriate Stimulus Control and Excessive Behavior

The judgment of whether a behavior is appropriate is based on several variables, as discussed in Chapters 1 and 2. Observers must consider the context in which a behavior occurs and their own values or biases. Some excessive behaviors may not be inappropriate by themselves but become targets for change when they are performed at the wrong time and in the wrong place (e.g., urinating in hallways, masturbating in public).

Excessive behaviors such as shouting, fighting, hoarding, complaining, and demanding help may be appropriate depending on the situation. However, the consequences which follow these behaviors can be difficult to manage, may become too intense, or may be hard to control outside an institutional setting. As a practical point, if a functional analysis reveals that consequences are controlling the behavior at a high rate, the behavior can be considered excessive. Response reduction techniques would then be appropriate.

The mental health professional must be careful to determine whether the behavior really is a significant problem for the client or merely annoys observers. It is also important to determine whether the behavior can be allowed (shaped) to continue in another setting or must be eliminated. To decide, the mental health professional must weigh the consequences of the behavior occurring in the present setting and the consequences that may occur in the alternative or discharge setting.

Assessment of Excessive Behavior

Because excessive behaviors can be observed and counted, assessment is fairly straightforward. Observers can readily establish frequency counts, length of occurrence, and intensity of the behaviors. Intensity can be measured by analyzing the impact that a target behavior has on the client's environment (e.g., number of items hoarded, distance furniture is moved, number of people disturbed). Observers can use their own ratings or a recording device to measure intensity.

Procedures for sampling excessive behaviors have been presented in a variety of reviews (see Goldfried & Sprafkin, 1974) and will not be covered here. The methods described in these reviews can be applied with little modification to an elderly population. We can, however, offer a few suggestions that might help observers develop more accurate assessments and more reliable problem definitions.

1. Extend the sampling to include antecedents and consequences of the target response. This approach provides information about the frequency of a behavior, the nature of the variables that maintain it, and a way of distinguishing between internal and external antecedents.
2. Set up the observations to minimize the influence of the investigator on the events being observed. Even in cases of severely demented clients, the presence of an observer may change the route clients take from one location to another, the amount of their self-stimulation or self-abuse, and their rates of compliance. Also, if staff behavior is influencing the rate of client responses, the investigator probably could record this only by observing staff and clients surreptitiously.
3. When appropriate, try out an intervention with the client. When clients are seen engaging in excessive behavior, the observer may wish to test various interventions before designing a formal program and training mediators. For example, if the client is shouting the same phrases or words over and over, the observer may move the person to another part of the room. This approach would test the

effects of external stimuli on the rate of the behavior and could pinpoint a simple intervention.

Treatment Considerations

The literature does not contain much detailed information on response reduction techniques for the aged population. Thus, the mental health professional interested in developing such techniques will have to build on others' experience with younger age groups. However, there is little reason to believe that these same techniques will not work equally well for elderly clients. Before describing the treatment, it may be helpful to discuss some of the issues involved in choosing the correct treatment procedure for various behaviors.

To identify the correct treatment, one must first specify the intensity, duration, and frequency of the behavior as well as its antecedents and consequences. For example, an episode of physical aggression may be triggered by another client's verbal or physical threats. Or the aggressive behavior may have been prompted by the client's paranoid delusions about another person's motives or actions. An environmental factor such as excessive noise or crowding could have caused the reaction. Or the stimulus may have been an unpleasant visit with a family member. In addition, pain or discomfort from physical conditions such as arthritis, headache, or constipation may also be a factor. Any of these antecedent variables may play a role in the client's excessive response.

Excessive behavior can also be maintained by the consequences that have followed the response in the past. For example, physical aggression may continue because it helped the client escape from an undesirable activity, from the unwanted attention of other clients, from being touched or restrained by the staff, or from verbal or social interventions. Excesses maintained by consequences are more likely to occur when there is little reinforcement for appropriate (incompatible) behavior.

Regardless of the treatment technique used, the strength and frequency of reinforcement should be high so that response reduction methods will have the appropriate impact on clients. If the level is low, the techniques will not be as successful since clients will perceive little difference between a low level of reinforcement and no reinforcement at all. As a result, response reduction techniques should always be combined with a strong positive reinforcement program.

Response Reduction Techniques

Interventions designed to reduce response rates in clients include distraction, extinction, differential reinforcement of other behavior, time out, correction, response cost, restriction, and aversive procedures. We will discuss each of these techniques emphasizing their practical application to problem behavior in the elderly.

Extinction

Extinction is the prevention of positive consequences that usually follow a particular behavior. This technique is the easiest to use, and the least invasive and restrictive intervention to reduce response rates. Withholding reinforcement is done by observers and must happen immediately after the behavior occurs to affect the response rate.

Though extinction requires the least effort on the part of observers, the technique may be difficult for mediators to apply consistently. They must ignore clients' repeated verbal abuse, threats, grandiose speech, racial slurs, and requests for help. In addition, while the original reinforcers may be withheld, others can take their place. Almost any behavior or change in the environment following the response may reinforce it. Any type of acknowledgment, whether the observer glares at the client, approaches the person, or laughs at the behavior, can increase the rate of response.

As can be seen, even "easy" techniques have their difficult side. For the mental health professional and paraprofessionals who wish to use extinction to reduce responses, we offer the following suggestions:

1. When the target behavior occurs, the observer should not establish eye contact with the client but look at a point beyond the individual. This approach removes the reinforcement of attracting someone's attention.
2. If a client becomes abusive, do not take the behavior personally or react in anger. Concentrate on something other than what the client is doing or saying to shut out the ongoing behavior. In this manner, the client is denied the reinforcement of engaging others in social interaction.
3. If you cannot block out the abusive behavior and find yourself becoming angry, fearful, or embarrassed, move away from the client. The important point is to withhold the reinforcing consequence of the client's behavior.

4. Be prepared to use another, more restrictive technique (e.g., time out) if the behavior escalates dramatically or becomes dangerous. You will have to exercise careful judgment about when to intervene with the alternative technique, but you should be ready to use it. You are removing a desired consequence and replacing it with one the client will not find reinforcing.

Extinction is an effective technique for the following target responses:

1. Verbal aggression and threats (not usually related to physical violence), cursing, and other abusive or inappropriate remarks.
2. Continual requests or demands for help when there is no real need for them.
3. Delusional or other forms of inappropriate speech that generally are not abusive but may be distracting or disturbing to others.
4. Yelling or shouting when it has been determined that the behavior is maintained in part by external consequences.

Time Out

Time out involves moving a client to an area where all reinforcers have been removed. This technique can help to ensure that positive consequences do not even accidentally follow an inappropriate behavior.

Time out may be administered two ways. Clients exhibiting the target behavior may be allowed to remain in the area but not take part in any ongoing (reinforcing) activities. Or the client may be moved to a separate location designated as a time-out area.

The second method is usually more appropriate for geriatric clients for two reasons. First, depriving clients of participation in an activity is effective only when the activity has some reinforcement value for the client. Since many elderly do not take part in activities, withholding this privilege may actually be reinforcing. Second, it may be difficult to get other clients to cooperate in the technique when the individual remains in the area. Accidental reinforcement from residents who wander by can limit the effectiveness of the procedure.

When prompting the client to enter the time-out area, follow these procedures:

1. Use as few prompts as possible; employ more active prompting only when passive guidance fails.
2. Provide as little reinforcement as possible when guiding the client to the area and during the time-out period. Briefly give the reason for the intervention (e.g., "You hit _____") and the criteria for release ("You can leave when you have been calm and quiet for 5 minutes"). Do not argue with clients, ask why they engaged in the behavior, or scold them. Such responses may simply reinforce the excessive behavior and reduce the effectiveness of time out.
3. Assign the shortest time-out period possible. In most cases, 5 minutes is sufficient. Any longer, and the treatment may not be effective. If after roughly 10 attempts at the shorter time period you do not get the desired results, extend the time gradually.
4. Tell the client when the criteria for release have been met. Releasing a client at the proper time is as important in controlling behavior as the prompt application of time out. This method helps establish reliable regulation and prevents the client from becoming unduly agitated in time out.
5. Even when clients show symptoms of advanced dementia that would seem to prevent them from gaining any benefit from time out, try the technique anyway. Only by using it and recording the results can you determine whether the technique (or any other intervention) can be effective. There is no foolproof way to predict when time out will or will not work.
6. Note the target behavior and selected intervention on a recording sheet and on the client's chart. The resulting data may be summarized in a graph or table.

Time out is an effective intervention for the following behaviors:

1. Physical aggression.
2. Sexual aggression.
3. Property damage.
4. Threats or other behavior that has often been followed by physical aggression.
5. Physical contact or aggression when attempting to leave the time-out area too soon.

CASE STUDY #3

A 66-year-old male with a diagnosis of schizophrenia, chronic undifferentiated type, had a history of aggression toward clients and staff of a mental institution. We treated his aggressive behavior by applying the usual 5 minutes in time out following each episode. The time-out room was devoid of any obvious reinforcers.

Yet even after approximately a year of such intervention, the client was still committing an average of four aggressive acts per week. Though a time-out procedure can take several months to effect a change in certain clients' behavior, in this case, the treatment team decided to change the strategy.

A functional analysis of the behavior revealed that most of the aggressive acts resulted in only mild consequences for the victims. The client would brush against others or grab lightly at them. For the most part, the behavior occurred near the time-out room. We hypothesized that the client found the room to be reinforcing.

The treatment team decided to use extinction for the mild physical contacts and reserve time out for major physical aggression. The time-out period was extended to 15 minutes. As a result of the change in treatment strategy, the aggression rate dropped to one episode per week. The seclusion rate (applied when the client left time out prematurely) dropped from 18 times in 12 months to 2 times in 5 months.

This case illustrates not only the benefits of a time-out procedure but also the importance of a functional analysis of behavior and flexibility in treatment design.

Correction

In correction a client must restore the environment to its original state prior to the individual's inappropriate behavior. When clients must perform some task they find disagreeable after a behavior, they are less likely to repeat the response.

To be effective, however, the correction task must be commensurate with the damage. For example, after voiding in an inappropriate place, the client should be prompted to clean the urine from the floor and change out of the wet clothes. This procedure can be used simultaneously with standard toilet training, positive practice, and stimulus enhancement/control techniques.

The procedure for applying the correction technique is as follows:

1. Once the target behavior occurs, the observer—using minimal prompts—should immediately prompt the client to restore the area. The client should complete as much of the behavioral chain as possible, taking out cleaning materials, cleaning the area, returning the materials, changing clothes, and the like.
2. Minimize any positive reinforcement of the behavior. Do not argue, grapple with the client, discuss the behavior, or in any way provide reinforcing consequences.
3. If the client refuses to comply even after being physically guided, institute the selected intervention for noncompliance. Should the client become combative during the correction procedure, institute time out. Only in rare cases is the client too confused to understand the chain of behaviors involved in correction. In such cases, discontinue the procedure if it fails to get results.
4. Write down the target behavior and intervention on the recording sheet and on the client's chart. Summarize the data in a graph or table.

Correction can be used for the following responses:

1. Spitting.
2. Spilling.
3. Some forms of inappropriate voiding/defecating.
4. Inappropriately moving furniture or other objects.

Response Cost

To change behavior, clients may be given tokens or items that they can "cash in" for various reinforcers (favorite food or activity) when they exhibit the appropriate response. Response cost involves taking these tokens or items away from a client following an inappropriate or excessive behavior. The technique is similar to a fine. Deducting tokens is the easiest way to administer response cost, although primary reinforcers may also be removed if necessary.

The procedure for applying response cost is as follows:

1. Establish a system in which various behaviors will result in the deduction of a specified number of tokens or items.

2. *Immediately* after the inappropriate target behavior, subtract the predetermined points or take away the favored item.
3. If the client refuses to yield the token or item, institute the intervention for noncompliance.
4. Should the client become abusive or combative, institute time out. Remember to remove all primary reinforcers from the client before the individual enters time out.

Response cost can be used effectively for these responses:

1. Failure to comply with a reasonable request.
2. Failure to attend therapy.
3. Possession of contraband items.
4. Stealing.
5. Violation of fire and safety rules.
6. Hoarding.

Restriction

Restriction is denying a client access to a favorite activity or area following an inappropriate behavior. Restrictions are designed to reduce future occurrences of the behavior.

The technique is relatively simple to apply, as outlined below:

1. Notify the client *immediately* of the restriction following an inappropriate behavior. Make sure all staff members involved know what action has been taken.
2. Do not threaten the client with the use of restriction for a precursor behavior. Apply restriction only when the target behavior occurs.
3. Remember that restricting clients' access to activities, particularly highly reinforcing ones, should be used with moderation. Multiple restrictions can cause clients to "give up" and reduce their level of participation in all activities.
4. Do not withhold essential items, activities, or areas from clients. Meals, liquids, toilet trips, and access to exercise areas cannot usually be restricted.
5. Withhold privileges that clients enjoy such as token store access, canteen trips, special recreation programs, and free time outside without a staff guide.
6. Record the target behavior and intervention and summarize the data.

Restrictions may be imposed following these behaviors:

1. Failure to comply with a reasonable request.
2. Severely disruptive behavior during or prior to a group activity.
3. Possession of contraband items.
4. Smoking in unauthorized areas.
5. Unauthorized departures from an area or the facility.

Differential Reinforcement of Other Behavior

Differential reinforcement of other behavior combines positive reinforcement for appropriate behavior with response reduction efforts. When interventions are applied, the client's new, appropriate responses should be followed by positive consequences. These new behaviors should be as incompatible with the target behavior as possible. Examples are provided in Table 4.1.

The procedure for differential reinforcement of other behavior (DRO) follows:

1. Specify the behavior to be reduced or eliminated and all the alternative (incompatible) behaviors that are to be positively reinforced.
2. Use extinction, time out, correction, response cost, or restriction when the inappropriate behavior occurs. For appropriate behavior, provide a predetermined reinforcer like tokens, favorite foods or activities, social interaction, and so on.
3. Note the target behavior and intervention and summarize data in a preferred format.

Differential reinforcement of other behavior can be applied to all excessive behaviors but is most effective for the following:

1. Self-abuse.
2. Rectal digging (a form of self-stimulation).
3. Stripping.
4. Hoarding.

It may also be used to reduce furniture relocation, although evidence supporting this application is scanty.

CASE STUDY #4
A 70-year-old male, hospitalized for 45 years with a diagnosis of chronic schizophrenia, exhibited extreme

TABLE 4.1
EXCESSIVE BEHAVIORS AND
APPROPRIATE (INCOMPATIBLE) RESPONSES

Excessive behavior	*Incompatible responses*
Head banging	Manipulation of stimulus material
Face slapping	Hand clapping
Demanding	Reasonable requests
Shouting	Whispering, singing
Complaints	Positive statements
Hoarding	Handing over materials
Furniture movement	Sitting
Shadowing	Sitting
Combativeness	Dancing, cooperative work
Verbal abuse	Giving compliments, neutral speech
Spitting	Whistling
Stripping	Dressing

hoarding behavior. The client would collect paper, linens, magazines, and other objects from trash cans, client lockers, and other areas on the hospital ward and grounds. Most of these items were stored in the client's locker, under his bed, under his pillow, and in his clothes. Outdoor access had to be limited because he would wander off from the supervised group to look for items he could collect. Attempts to prevent this behavior often led to physical aggression on the client's part.

A volume measure—a cardboard cylinder—was designed to establish a baseline rate of hoarding. The cylinder was marked off in inches. The items the client collected were placed in the cylinder and two measures were taken per day for 11 days of baseline. An intervention was then designed to reduce the hoarding. It consisted of verbal praise and a cigarette when the amount of hoarded items dropped below a certain height established as a criterion.

During the baseline measurement, the height of the material in the cylinder averaged 11 inches. After 13 days of intervention, in which the criterion was continually reduced, the amount of material hoarded dropped to 3 1/2 inches. The client stopped digging in trash cans altogether. Follow-up after 2 months showed that he was no longer hoarding items of any measurable quantity.

This case is an example of differential reinforcement of other behavior—in this instance, a non-hoarding behavior.

Distraction

Distraction involves shifting a client's attention from one behavior or activity to another. It does not have as much supporting evidence in the literature for its effectiveness as do other response reduction techniques. Yet it can be useful in reducing certain behaviors for badly confused clients whose excessive responses are unacceptably high. When excessive behavior is secondary to delirium or dementia, distraction may be the only possible intervention.

The procedure is summarized below:

1. When the target behavior occurs (wandering, arguing, escalating verbal abuse, delusional speech), the client should be prompted to engage in an alternative response (sitting, conversing with others on a neutral topic, talking about something concrete).
2. Use extinction for inappropriate statements/behavior and deliver reinforcement when positive or neutral behavior occurs.

Aversive Procedures

Aversive procedures often involve engaging the client in some type of forced activity. Several aversive techniques like overcorrection, contingent restraint, forced relaxation, or the application of unpleasant stimuli are available to the mental health professional. However, before they can be applied, the investigator must be sure that the patients' rights are considered and that various legal and ethical requirements are satisfied. The program designer should do the following:

1. Demonstrate that the behavior is clearly dangerous to the client or others.
2. Show that other, less intrusive treatments have not reduced the target behavior.
3. Carefully train all staff members to apply the program. If various kinds of apparatus are used in aversive proce-

dures, staff should be trained in how they work, how to use them safely, what side-effects may occur, and how to record results.

4. The apparatus, application, and progress of treatment should be checked periodically by a review board comprised of knowledgeable individuals who are not directly involved in the client's care.

Aversive procedures that have been used successfully with other client populations and that often work with elderly clients include the following:

Overcorrection. In this method, the investigator or staff prompt the client not only to restore the environment (correction) but also to clean or restore a larger area than the one damaged. For example, a client who throws a piece of furniture would be prompted to put the object back in its original place and also to straighten and clean all the furniture in the room.

Contingent restraint. When contingent restraint is used, a client's movements are partially or totally restricted by mechanical or physical means. The technique is applied after other methods of handling an inappropriate behavior have failed. Noncontingent restraint, such as ordered by a physician to prevent a client from suffering injury, is not considered an aversive procedure. To be effective, contingent restraint must immediately follow a target behavior.

Forced relaxation or forced effort. In this method, the staff or other caretaker prompts the client to discontinue a target behavior by engaging the person either in exercise or relaxation techniques whenever the behavior occurs.

Application of aversive stimuli. The target behavior is discouraged by applying a painful or noxious stimulus (e.g., shock, hot sauce, unpleasant tasting liquid, loud noise) whenever the behavior occurs. This method is one way to prevent self-abuse, rumination, and other responses that are difficult to reduce or eliminate. However, the technique must be applied with great care to prevent it from becoming abusive rather than aversive.

When response reduction techniques are employed, the mental health professional must ensure that new, more desirable responses are reinforced. As targeted behaviors are eliminated, neutral, appropriate, or independent behaviors must take their place. If the professional works to provide a reinforcing environment, accidental support for inappropriate behavior can be avoided. To do anything else would be ethically and procedurally unsound. The basic principle, then, is never attempt to reduce target behavior without reinforcing either alternative or new appropriate behavior.

Treatment

Treatments commonly used for many excessive behaviors among the elderly population are listed in Table 4.2. In general, excessive behaviors exhibited by all clients will be followed, at least initially, by one of these consequences. When the data indicate that a particular behavior is not being reduced after several weeks, other techniques or modifications must be applied.

Although little outcome research has been reported on applying reduction techniques to change the elderly client's excessive behaviors, the few existing studies that have been done have shown that such interventions can be very successful. Rosberger and MacLean (1983) reduced multiple excessive responses in clients such as kicking, tripping others, and throwing objects by combining reduction and reinforcement of alternative behavior. Staff members of a nursing home carried out the differential reinforcement program.

Haley (1983) reduced anger and multiple complaints in a 71-year-old female with a history of paranoid schizophrenia. The author conducted eight one-hour sessions using a combination of modeling, relaxation training, reinforcement, positive self-statement training, and role playing. Complaints of arthritic pain by an 80-year-old female were reduced 71% through six sessions of electromyography biofeedback training (Boczkowski, 1984). The client also was able to cut the dosage of her arthritis medicine by half while increasing flexion and grip strength.

Since the behavioral program has been in place at our geriatric facility, rates of physical and verbal aggression have begun to decline. Physical aggression has been reduced by 25% and verbal aggression by 44% over the same period the previous year (Hussian & Yore, 1984). However, the trend has been reversing lately as more chronic clients are admitted.

Special Considerations

The following considerations should be kept in mind when using response reduction techniques across a population or for individuals.

TABLE 4.2
INTERVENTIONS FOR BEHAVIORAL EXCESSES

Problem behavior	Intervention(s)
1. Minor (less than 1 minute) verbal abusiveness, threats, cursing	Extinction
2. Major (more than 1 minute) verbal abusiveness, threats, cursing	Dorm, chair, or corner time out
3. Physical aggression, threats associated with subsequent physical aggression	Room time out
4. Sexual abuse	Room time out
5. Purposive urination or defecation in inappropriate area	Correction
6. Hoarding, trash digging	DRO and/or response cost
7. Repetitive demands, complaints, requests for medication (no organic etiology)	Extinction
8. Refusals to comply	Restriction
9 Shadowing	Distraction, DRO
10. Furniture movement	DRO (suggested)
11. Self-stimulation	DRO (suggested)

1. Conduct a sufficient number of baseline observations prior to the intervention. To do so may mean permitting the client to engage in the behavior, making sure, however, that it does not endanger others. Establish the baseline frequency and convert this to an average (i.e., episodes per hour, per day, or per shift). Continue the frequency count throughout treatment and, if possible, after treatment has been discontinued.
2. As mentioned earlier, always provide a reinforcing environment and directly reinforce alternative (incompatible) responses.
3. If your facility is not connected with a larger system (university, state institution) consider establishing a review board or committee. Its function would be to evaluate *all* response reduction proposals and not simply the aversive programs. When aversive interventions may be necessary, the board or committee should consider such questions as

staff training, timing of the techniques, clients' rights and consent, progress reviews, and criteria for treatment termination.

4. As a rule, use the less invasive reduction techniques first before progressing to stricter methods. For example, when treating a client who is verbally aggressive, try extinction first, then progress to "corner" time out in the same area. If the client attempts to leave time out and is physically aggressive in the process, move the individual to "room" time out away from the area. The time-out room should be used primarily as a consequence of physical aggression.

   More invasive procedures can also be used if a less strict technique fails to reduce the target behavior. If response cost, for example, does not reduce a client's non-compliance over several weeks, the clinician would be justified in progressing to restriction methods.

5. Re-evaluate response reduction programs at least once a year. Incorporate new techniques as they are validated in the literature. Make it a point to incorporate less restrictive or more positive programs as they become available. Consider shortening time-out periods and using more minimal prompts to promote alternative and independent behavior in clients.

5

Problems of Stimulus Control

Inappropriate behavior may result from insufficient or inappropriate stimuli rather than simply from the relationship between the behavior and its reinforcing consequences. In certain situations, behavior is viewed as inappropriate when performed out of context. For example, voiding is a perfectly appropriate behavior if it occurs in the presence of certain stimuli and in a certain order:

1. Awareness of the need to void.
2. Moving toward the appropriate receptacle or requesting that one be brought.
3. Freeing the genitals from clothing.
4. Placing the genitals reasonably close to an appropriate receptacle.
5. Having the urine enter the receptacle.

However, if the chain is completed successfully but in the wrong context (in the middle of a crowded room), the behavior is no longer acceptable. As discussed in Chapters 1 and 2, any analysis of behavior is incomplete if contextual variables are not considered. In the voiding example above, the entire chain may occur in the toilet or in the hallway with an identical outcome from the *client's* standpoint. However, from the *caretaker's* point of view, the consequences will be quite different.

The use of functional analysis is critical in discovering the role that insufficient or inappropriate stimulus control plays in maintaining an inappropriate behavior. Interventions for such behaviors may be different from those used to reduce excess responses or to increase deficit responding. In the example above, for instance, inappropriate voiding might be maintained by positive consequences (i.e., attention, laughter, tactile stimulation when clothes are changed). In such cases, the selected treatments, such as correction, response cost, or an aversive program, would be designed to reduce response rates. On the other hand, if the behavior is in fact the result of perceptual and/or cognitive errors, using response reduction therapies would be ineffective and even unethical.

Contextual Cues and Antecedent Variables

When contextual cues and antecedent variables are considered in behavior analysis, the results can provide several benefits for staff, mental health professionals, and clients.

1. Such an approach reduces the concern over deciding which target behaviors are appropriate for response reduction techniques. Stimulus enhancement and control therapies are designed to permit behaviors to occur in predetermined locations or times without necessarily changing the rate of a behavior.
2. Stimulus enhancement and control procedures usually require less staff involvement, thus reducing training time and avoiding inconsistent applications of treatments.
3. The procedures can be used with other methods like shaping, extinction, and differential reinforcement for other types of behavior. Clients who show severe cognitive and/or perceptual dysfunction may need stimulus enhancement and control techniques to effect appropriate changes and facilitate maintenance of new responses.
4. Stimuli used for training or discrimination purposes can be designed during the planning phases of a geriatric facility (Koncelik, 1976) or added later at minimal cost. Materials generally involve only cardboard cutouts, contact paper, adhesive symbols and labels, and other dispensable reinforcers.
5. Once in place, stimulus control symbols can remain on display to enhance maintenance of client responses. The stimuli can also be moved to other areas to help clients generalize their treatment gains.

The discussion of antecedent modification can be divided into two parts: stimulus enhancement techniques and stimulus control training.

Stimulus Enhancement

Mental health professionals will not find a great deal in the literature on using stimulus enhancement techniques with elderly populations. However, some studies have shown that auditory cues to prompt activity participation (Quattrochi-Tubin & Jason, 1980) and the presence of stimulus materials to increase interaction (McClannahan & Risley, 1975) have been effective.

Pollock and Liberman (1974) used a combination of bladder control techniques and stimulus enhancement to reduce episodes of incontinence in elderly patients. For one difficult dementia patient, the authors used colored tape on the floor to help the individual find the appropriate toilet and to shape differential responding.

To improve ward-orienting responses in dementia patients, Hanley (1981) used three-dimensional signs and verbal orientation to help clients find their way around the ward. Peterson, Knapp, Rosen, and Pither (1977) noted the effects of different seating arrangements on social interaction among elderly clients. These authors found that the frequency of social interactions could be increased by placing chairs in a circle rather than in linear or oval arrangements.

Bakos, Bozic, Chapin, and Neuman (1980) of Architecture-Research-Construction in Cleveland studied the impact of changing design elements on clients' agitation, cognitive abilities, and feelings of loneliness. They observed patients (average age 69) in a psychogeriatric facility by using time sampling, behavioral mapping, interviews, the Philadelphia Geriatric Center Morale Scale, WAIS subtests, and an attitudinal scale at baseline and post-design change. Some of the design changes were suggested by one half of the residents during small group meetings which focused on environmental barriers and aids. The authors found that dividing facilities into functionally different activity areas increased the amount of staff time spent in the day room with the residents and decreased the time spent in the nursing station. The social interaction among residents also increased with the new arrangement. Interestingly enough, residents who participated in the design groups showed more significant gains in functional behavior than did residents who benefited from the changes but did not participate in the decision-making process.

More controlled studies are needed to establish which design and stimulus components are most effective in shaping or rerouting certain types of behavior. However, it does appear that using certain "supernormal" stimuli in the environment may increase appropriate functioning in the elderly client. Certainly, such important behavioral categories as activity participation, exercise and recreation, social interactions, and appropriate voiding and sexual behavior can be affected through the use of enhancement techniques.

Stimulus enhancement also can be used to encourage or discourage other responses such as compliance with therapy or taking medication, smoking only in designated areas, use of others' personal property, safe ambulation, and appropriate entry into privilege areas. Table 5.1 lists the behaviors and the appropriate enhancement techniques for each one.

To illustrate functional analysis and the effective use of stimulus enhancement, we will describe a problem behavior—trespass—that occurs frequently in institutions.

Trespass

Trespass is defined as nonprompted entry into another person's private area or into an unauthorized area. The behavior is not unique to older inpatients but occurs commonly in psychiatric inpatient settings. Trespassing usually involves the use of another client's locker or bed.

Trespassing is a valid target for change for several reasons. In inpatient settings, this behavior often leads to physical aggression when owners observe the trespass or the results of someone using their possessions. The trespasser may also be injured if the area of trespass is dangerous such as a shop area or kitchen where machinery is kept.

To select the best intervention, the mental health professional must conduct a careful functional analysis. The observed behavior may be maintained by consequential variables or poor stimulus control. The mental health professional should keep the following considerations in mind when analyzing the behavior.

1. Trespassing may be purposeful behavior designed to gain some material goods or advantage from the rightful owner. As a result, the behavior may simply be a way of engaging in other problem behaviors such as stealing or sexual behavior. In this case, the behavior is maintained by periodically acquiring items or advantages. Careful observation should reveal the existence of such reinforcers.

TABLE 5.1
BEHAVIORS AMENABLE TO
STIMULUS ENHANCEMENT

Behavioral category	Nature of enhancement
Activity participation	Prompt
Interaction with stimulus materials	Prompt
Exercise and recreation	Prompt, area definition
Social interactions	Prompt
Appropriate toileting and sexual behavior	Area definition, route demarcation
Medication and therapy compliance	Prompt, area definition
Use of smoking areas	Area definition
Ownership (locker and bed)	Area definition
Safe ambulation	Route demarcation
Access to prohibited areas	Area definition
Access to privilege areas	Area definition, reinforcer
Access to extinction areas	Area definition, avoidance
Personnel functions	Service definition

2. Trespassing may also be the result of deficient stimulus control during ambulation (wandering). Clients may not see signs warning them to stay out of the area or may not realize they are in someone else's room.

Trespassing can be handled by intervening at either the antecedent or consequent points in the behavioral model.

CASE STUDY #5

A 71-year-old male resident of a long-term care center, who was diagnosed with senile dementia (primary degenerative dementia, senile onset), spent considerable time trespassing into other clients' rooms and going through their belongings. This behavior often provoked angry reactions from the other residents.

A functional analysis of this annoying and frequently dangerous behavior revealed that the client seldom took any items and never attempted sexual contact. When not engaged in trespassing, he exhibited a high level of behavior that appeared to be independent of observable stimuli (e.g., talking to himself, inappropriate voiding).

It was also noted that, except for position cues, the doors to clients' rooms were not marked.

We moved the client from his room in the middle of the wing to another room and taped a bright red rectangle on his door. For 1 week the client was physically prompted to return to his new room whenever he was observed trespassing. Each time, the red marker was pointed out to him.

Within 3 weeks the client was no longer trespassing into other residents' rooms and was not involved in any disputes with them. The extinction of trespassing continued for over 1 year until physical illness required relocating the client to a nursing home wing within the facility.

Antecedent intervention. The behavior could be prevented by restricting the client's movement or access to unauthorized areas. However, problems with this approach are obvious. Restricting a client's movement, while preventing trespassing, also inhibits other appropriate responses such as ambulation, social interaction, and other necessary forms of stimulation. In addition, response prevention does not allow the client to learn new associations. If it is possible to train or re-train the person in appropriate responding, the trespassing behavior should be allowed to occur and its course, route, or direction shaped by observers. Finally, fire codes and other regulations may make it impossible to restrict access in some settings.

It may also be possible to permit the precursor behavior to continue while eliminating the act of trespass. In this case, stimulus enhancement (or stimulus control) can be beneficial. For example, we have used color-coded sleeping areas and personalized symbols successfully in our facility to reduce trespass without limiting ambulation. For other situations, it may be feasible to match the color code with the wristband of the client, giving the individual a constant referent.

Consequent intervention. When trespass seems to be maintained by contingent positive reinforcement rather than as a result of disorientation, the therapist should consider changing the reinforcing consequences. Interventions that may prove effective include response cost, replacing the stolen articles (restitution), restoring any damage (correction), overcorrection, and restriction from a favorite activity. For treatment to be effective, the costs imposed for the act of trespassing must be greater than or equal to the reinforcement value of the items or advantages gained from the behavior.

Special Guidelines for Stimulus Enhancement

The following guidelines may be helpful in developing stimulus enhancement programs for elderly clients.

1. Use simple, straightforward stimulus displays. Simple colors, lines, and symbols usually are more effective than complicated directions or written signs.
2. Minimize irrelevant or distracting stimuli in the display. Adding multiple stimuli and irrelevant information may render the entire display useless for controlling behavior. Clients cannot follow directions if they have trouble distinguishing them from other elements in the display.
3. Emphasize figure/ground or figure/background contrast. Changes in many elderly clients' eyesight require the use of high-contrast symbols against low-intensity backgrounds. For example, you might use bright orange or yellow against a navy blue or brown background.
4. Keep the instructions simple and easy to follow. The clients should be able to discover the intention of the symbols or cues quickly. For instance, special codes that mark locations and that require clients to process information in several steps will not be very effective. Instead, use simpler symbols such as a knife and fork for a dining area or red and green access symbols.
5. Provide written or oral announcements 10 to 15 minutes before an activity or event that clients want to attend. This allows them time to prepare for the event. Announcing programs too far in advance generally is not effective since clients may forget or confuse the time and place with other activities.
6. Arrange seating to enhance social interaction and activity participation. Consider using small clusters of tables and chairs in large rooms, circular seating at meals and during activities, and separate areas for various activities.
7. Post prominent reminders of daily activity schedules to remind clients and their visitors when specific programs are taking place.

8. Consider using individualized room or bed markers to distinguish one room from another. This technique helps alleviate the problem in many institutions of seemingly endless corridors with indistinguishable doors. The construction of these markers can be part of a planned activity for the clients.

In some cases, clients' level of functioning is so low that the clinician must expend considerable effort introducing special stimuli to clients in order to shape their responses. Caregivers must then use stimulus control techniques.

Stimulus Control

Stimulus control involves pairing a cue with a reinforcer or some negative event to shape a client's response, then gradually presenting the cue alone. For some clients, using bright, colorful stimuli is not enough to shape appropriate behavior. These clients need more than passive environmental interventions for the following reasons.

1. Clients in the middle-to-late stages of a progressive dementia require techniques that include basic training in associating stimulus and response to increase their chances of acquiring and maintaining desired behaviors. These clients often exhibit extreme deficits in attention span, verbal abilities, and other functions, which rule out interventions depending on verbal prompts or setting rules.
2. The more time clients spend in an institution, the less attention they appear to pay to environmental cues, possibly because the cues become habituated. Also, clients may not be reinforced for following routines or cues and may simply move through the environment passively.
3. The normal sensory and peripheral changes of aging, which worsen with disease, often reduce clients' ability to respond to standard or even "supernormal" stimuli. As a result, clients may need intensive training, through stimulus discrimination, to bring various behaviors under the control of selected stimuli.

If these three reasons apply in a client's situation, a "supernormal" stimulus may need to be paired with immediate consequences (i.e., positive reinforcement, extinction, or aversive techniques) during training sessions. This special stimulus can be placed in the environment where a client's approach or avoidance behavior is desired.

Stimulus control is particularly effective for treating behaviors that are not in themselves inappropriate but become unacceptable in the wrong place and time. Other responses, such as those classified as deficits or excesses, can be modified by combining stimulus control with more traditional behavioral techniques. In the following sections, we discuss two behaviors, wandering and inappropriate sexual behavior, that appear fairly often in geriatric facilities and at home. They illustrate the effective use of stimulus control techniques, which incorporate parts of other behavioral methods.

Wandering

Wandering refers to ambulation that occurs independently of the usual environmental cues (e.g., announcement to attend an activity, invitation from another resident to visit, attending meals, and the like). Ambulation, per se, is not usually targeted for change, unless it is drug-induced akathisia or restlessness. Rather, ambulation into hazardous or unauthorized areas will be the target behavior since it may result in accidents, inappropriate entries, trespass and possible physical aggression, and efforts to sedate or restrain the client.

The mental health professional must conduct a functional analysis of an individual's wandering before choosing an intervention. Casual observation may lead one to believe that all types of ambulation are alike, particularly in the confines of a ward. However, a study by Hussian and Davis (1983) suggests that this is not the case.

These authors reported a study of 13 residents of a geriatric unit of a state mental institution. Eight of the residents were male and five were female, with one female client aged 53 and all other clients 60 years of age or older. Four trained observers, using floor plans of the wards, observed the clients' movements in three or four 20-minute intervals. The observers recorded the following information:

1. The routes taken by each client.
2. The number of times clients turned the knob on a door.
3. The amount of self-stimulation that took place.
4. The percentage of time spent ambulating alone versus with others.

5. The number of times the clients asked to leave the floor.
6. The percentage of exit doors touched.
7. The total time spent ambulating during the 20-minute intervals.
8. Several other client characteristics.

As a result of these observations, four ambulation patterns emerged, each correlated with different variables. The data are summarized in Table 5.2.

The ambulation patterns can be divided best as follows:

1. *Akathisiacs.* This type of wandering is represented by the first two clients in Table 5.2. They had been hospitalized longer than the others and were receiving higher doses of neuroleptic medication. These clients tended to ambulate more often within the 20-minute intervals and showed little interest either in leaving the ward or in self-stimulatory activity.
2. *Exit seekers.* Clients three and four in Table 5.2, who were admitted the most recently, could be labeled as exit seekers. They asked to leave the ward 5 to 10 times more frequently than other clients (e.g., "Open the door, I gotta see my wife" or "Unlock the door for me; give me a ride home"). They also tried the exit doors more often than those leading to storage areas or offices, even though the latter doors were more numerous. The time they spent in ambulation varied, and they did not engage in self-stimulation. Incidentally, as length of stay increased, the number of exit doors and the number of total doors touched dropped sharply.
3. *Modelers.* Clients five through eight tended to ambulate only in the presence of another ambulator. They tended to touch door knobs only briefly and showed little self-stimulatory behavior. Their ambulation times varied according to the time spent with another ambulator.
4. *Self-stimulators.* The last five clients' ambulation patterns are best described as self-stimulatory. When these clients touched the door knobs, they tended to turn them repeatedly, perhaps receiving auditory and tactile stimulation. These clients also exhibited other forms of stereotypy such as hand-clapping or rubbing objects. They showed no preference for exit doors over other doors on the ward.

TABLE 5.2
ETIOLOGY OF WANDERING

Client	Group[1]	Medications[2]	Length of hospitalization	Average # of turns	Self-stimulation per 20'	Time alone	% Exit doors	Duration[3]
1	A	150 Serentil	21 months	1.5	5.5	50	0.12	Long
2	A	300 Mellaril	77 months	2.2	0	98	12.40	Long
3	ES	2 Haldol	2 months	2.5	0	99	94.50	Medium
4	ES	4 Haldol	5 days	1.3	0	100	100.00	Short
5	M	75 Mellaril	5 months	1.0	1.5	14	25.00	Medium
6	M	100 Mellaril	8 months	1.3	6.3	40	0.44	Medium
7	M	0.5 Haldol	3 months	2.0	0.5	2	0	Long
8	M	6 Navane	13 months	2.8	1.8	9	28.0	Long
9	SS	50 Mellaril	5 months	17.8	34.5	50	34.4	Long
10	SS	1 Haldol	6 months	6.5	63.2	95	.1	Medium
11	SS	100 Mellaril	14 months	11.7	30.2	97	.7	Long
12	SS	25 Mellaril	10 months	7.8	13.0	100	24.8	Medium
13	SS	1 Haldol	7 months	9.5	22.0	99	58.0	Medium

[1]A = Akathisiacs   ES = Exit Seekers   M = Modelers   SS = Self-Stimulators
[2]Daily doses
[3]Short = One third or less of total time observed was spent in ambulation.
Medium = One third to two thirds of total time observed was spent in ambulation.
Long = Two thirds to 100% of total time observed was spent in ambulation.

This study should make clinicians aware of the different patterns that occur even in apparently simple behaviors.

If a failure of appropriate stimulus control appears to be maintaining wandering, one might use stimulus control training to modify clients' ambulation patterns. In one study, Hussian (1982) consistently paired two colored stimuli with two distinctly different consequences, one positive and one negative. The author used the technique to modify potentially hazardous wandering in three long-term care residents (mean age, 73.4 years, and mean hospitalization, 13 months). An orange cardboard cutout stimulus was associated with the delivery of applesauce to clients whose wandering was a problem. A blue cardboard stimulus was associated with a loud noise.

Once a preference for attending to the orange symbol was shown and avoidance of the blue symbol was evident, these colored symbols were posted on the wards. The blue symbol was placed in areas where ambulation was discouraged while the orange symbol was placed in areas where ambulation was encouraged and could be monitored.

Behavioral mapping of the residents' movements showed that clients who had undergone training ambulated at about the same rate and duration but made fewer entries into dangerous areas. As a result, stimulus control training did not reduce ambulation per se—clients continued to enjoy relatively free range of motion—but did reduce the negative consequences of ambulation.

Clients selected for training in this case were quite debilitated and required extreme measures for treatment. Other, simpler techniques can also be used to modify wandering, depending, of course, on the pattern exhibited and degree of clients' cognitive impairment. Some potential management techniques that can be used with the ambulation patterns, that are observed in the Hussian and Davis (1983) report are summarized in Table 5.3.

These interventions are based partly on logical extensions of the analyses of behavior drawn from the Hussian (1982) study described above. Some verification of the interventions, while not extensive, has been observed in our facility. It is also possible that stimulus enhancement alone can decrease potentially dangerous wandering. Or clients may be allowed to move about the facility only when they can be monitored closely.

TABLE 5.3
POTENTIAL MANAGEMENT TECHNIQUES
FOR WANDERING

Type of ambulator	Technique
Akathisiacs	Stimulus Control: Shape ambulation to a circumscribed area.
	Drug Change: Change or reduce neuroleptic.
	Observe ambulation.
Exit-seekers	Extinction: Continued non-reinforcement at exit doors.
	Stimulus Control: Shape ambulation to a circumscribed area.
Modelers	Stimulus Control: Shape ambulation to a circumscribed area.
	Observe ambulation.
	No intervention: When successful with other wanderers.
Self-stimulators	Stimulus Control: Shape ambulation to a circumscribed area.
	Sensory Extinction: Reduce feedback from knob turning.
	DRO: Provide sensory reinforcement for other responses.

Inappropriate Sexual Behavior

Inappropriate sexual behavior is sexual behavior that occurs at inappropriate times and places or that is forced on other residents or staff. Such behaviors include masturbating in public areas, fondling, and sexual contact with others at the wrong time and place. This behavior can be particularly difficult to manage in institutions and at home. Generally, however, it is more bothersome to the observers than to the clients who instigate it.

Caregivers and professionals may forget that elderly clients have no reason not to exhibit sexual behavior even though they are advanced in years and may reside on wards with only members of the same sex. As a result, decisions about when such behavior is appropriate can become difficult. Some of the difficulty can be circumvented, however, by viewing the behavior as a problem of context rather than being intrinsically unacceptable. A stimulus control approach can work well within this perspective.

Hussian (1982) used stimulus control to reduce public masturbation in a 64-year-old long-term care facility male resident.

The client was trained successfully to distinguish between the consequences for public versus private masturbation. Previous attempts to modify his public sexual behavior had included rule setting, positive reinforcement for alternative behavior, and restrictions following the inappropriate behavior. These attempts failed to bring about any change.

The stimulus control intervention involved interrupting the client's masturbatory behavior when it occurred in the lobby or in front of the nursing station. The same behavior was allowed to reach its natural outcome when it occurred in the privacy of the resident's bedroom. The differential outcome was reinforced by placing a bright orange symbol on the wall above the resident's bed. Without some type of stimulus, the client apparently could not distinguish between a public and private setting with their different contingencies. With the orange symbol in place, however, the average number of public masturbatory acts dropped from four to zero while private masturbation increased from a baseline rate of three per eight-hour day shift to a little over five. No episodes of public masturbation occurred during the follow-up conducted one week after treatment ended, and the symbols were removed with no return of the public behavior.

As can be seen from this example, different consequences were associated with the behavior occurring in two settings. Aversive consequences were associated with public masturbation and the absence of an orange symbol, while positive consequences followed private masturbation and the presence of an orange stimulus.

In such instances, the only ethically defensible option for caregivers is not to eliminate the behavior. It is unlikely that any long-term care facility could offer an appropriate alternative response. Rather, the emphasis should be on changing the setting in which the behavior is allowed to occur. Both client and staff achieve their desired outcomes. The client is permitted to continue the same behavior, and the staff and visitors can conduct their business without feeling offended.

The basic procedures for stimulus control training are as follows:

1. Conduct a functional analysis of the target behavior. The results should indicate whether the inappropriate behavior is occurring because of the consequences that maintain it or is happening independently of the consequences.

In the latter case, the clinician should look for antecedent controlling factors.

2. If the behavior seems to occur independently of its consequences and is not intrinsically aberrant, the target behavior should be specified in measurable terms. For example, if the problem involves inappropriate sexual behavior, it should be defined carefully with all the inclusions and exclusions noted and confirmed by those who will be intervening.

   If masturbation is the target behavior, the clinician must specify the *context* within which the behavior occurs (e.g., in the bathroom stall with the door closed, in the client's bedroom) and the *topography* of the response (e.g., the hand must be in contact with the genitals and showing movement for longer than 5 seconds). The observer should exclude accidental contacts between the client's hands and genitals as well as contacts inherent during normal bodily functions such as urinating or bathing. On the other hand, it might be important to include contact between the genitals and pieces of furniture, objects, and other clients as part of the target behavior.

   The target for change, and any acceptable alternatives, should be clearly specified. More than one person may be involved in the intervention whether at home or in a geriatric facility, and the treatment must be applied consistently if it is to succeed.

3. Choose symbols that can be clearly seen and easily understood. They should stand out from the surrounding background and convey their message simply and vividly.

4. If external sources of reinforcement must be provided to encourage and strengthen alternative behavior, make sure they are appropriate to the client's level of functioning and individual preferences. Traditional reinforcers may not provide clients with sufficient motivation.

5. At times it may be necessary to select an aversive stimulus to be paired with an avoidance symbol. The clinician must be sure to clear the choice of aversive stimulus with the proper channels to satisfy ethical and legal considerations. This stimulus need not be painful or intense, particularly when another symbol is being paired with something pleasant and the two consequences are alternated. Some

aversive consequences include loud, brief noises; mild and brief physical restraint; and removal of a positive reinforcer.

6. In a quiet setting, seat the client across from the clinician and present the symbol to be associated with the positive behavior. When the client has focused attention on it, respond by saying, "That's good" and present the positive reinforcer immediately. Remove the symbol and present the stimulus to be associated with avoidance. When the client attends to this symbol, provide the chosen aversive stimulus. Alternate the symbols so they are presented an equal number of times.

7. If it is difficult to focus clients' attention on the symbols during training sessions, try gently guiding their hand to the symbol and/or turning their head so they are looking at the stimulus.

8. After several trials of alternation, present the two symbols *at the same time*. Each time the client touches or looks at one of the symbols, follow with the appropriate consequence. Continue this stage of the procedure several trials beyond the point at which the client achieves a 100% preference for the symbol associated with positive or nonaversive consequences. This overtraining prolongs the desirable behavior and seems to help clients apply the new response to the actual situation.

9. Place the symbol(s) in the appropriate areas. The positive symbol should be in areas where the target behavior is allowed to occur. The symbol associated with aversive consequences or nonreinforcement should be in the areas where the behavior is to be discouraged.

10. Continue to monitor the client after the symbols are in place to determine if the client still responds to them appropriately. If not, the clinician should attempt to discover the problem. There may have been insufficient training trials, the symbols may be poorly placed, other stimuli may be exerting stronger attractions on the client's attention, or other reinforcers may be more powerful than the ones provided by the clinician.

Even after successfully training a client in stimulus control techniques, the clinician may need to conduct further training trials periodically. These may consist of the clinician pointing out the different symbols in the environment to the client and delivering the appropriate consequences. During this modified training, the clinician should make sure that the client is prompted to respond to the *symbol* and not to the *objects* such as the bed, toilet, or door, since these objects were not the controlling stimuli in the first place.

However, once the behavior comes under stimulus control, the symbols might be gradually faded or removed in favor of the naturally occurring objects. This transfer is particularly important in the following instances:

1. The client shows some improvement in overall cognitive functioning. Such improvement may be the case when poor stimulus control and initial confusion were caused by an acute organic problem which has since been cleared up through medical treatment.

2. The client is to be discharged to another facility in which these symbols and training methods are not likely to be used or employed consistently. If the client remains too confused for the fading procedure to be attempted, the clinician should at least give the new facility the symbols and training format used (see Appendix D, Discharge Program: Wandering).

Special Considerations for Stimulus Control

Clinicians should be aware of several special considerations when designing and implementing these programs.

1. The therapist must take care not to use symbols for one client that might interfere with symbols designed for other clients. For example, if an orange sphere is used to reduce wandering in one client, it should not also be used to reduce inappropriate voiding in another client. Since there are only a limited number of symbols that can be used and a limited number of places to put them in a ward or unit, the clinician should work with only a few clients at a time.

2. The symbols used for stimulus control within a unit must be clearly distinguished from any existing stimulus enhancement cues in place. If certain colors have been employed to help shape group responses, those colors should not be used for individual stimulus control programs.

3. In institutional settings, particularly those caring for both demented and general psychiatric clients, make sure the symbols are constructed of durable materials and fixed securely to structures. If possible, they should be placed out of clients' reach. Otherwise the symbols may be destroyed or altered. Clients may try to eat them, set fire to the symbols, or use them for self-stimulation. Construct the symbols out of contact paper, wood, or metal and nail or screw them into place. Posterboard, tape, and paper are too easily removed, ripped, or marked over with crayons, pens, or other drawing materials.

Stimulus enhancement and control procedures have been used effectively for some problem behaviors, even though more basic research is needed before the methods can be embraced without reservation. As noted in this chapter, few controlled studies have been conducted to explore the effectiveness of such procedures, and none examined the impact of treatment components on client behavior. Though Woods (1980) has shown that similar procedures have modified responses in autistic children, the widespread use of stimulus enhancement and control techniques for behavioral problems in the elderly client population requires much more study and evaluation. It is hoped that more investigators will look into the subject in the near future.

6

Special Considerations in Inpatient Settings

Most of the treatments described in this book for behavioral deficits, excesses, and problems of stimulus control can be applied readily in inpatient settings. In fact, with their better inservice educational opportunities, multiple care providers, more consistent and continuous monitoring, and greater range of disciplines represented, inpatient facilities generally provide better settings for program application than do either private homes or outpatient clinics.

There are, however, a few characteristics of these inpatient settings that can make behavioral intervention difficult. The main problem involves the clinician's need for cooperation from staff members and other caregivers who often have a wide variety of educational and experiential backgrounds. Relying on individuals who are neither psychologists nor mental health professionals to administer and evaluate individual and group programs carries certain inherent, though not irremediable, difficulties.

In this chapter, we will discuss some of the potential problems that mental health professionals may encounter when applying behavior therapy techniques in inpatient settings.

Staff Cooperation and Consistency

As pointed out in Chapter 2, effective behavior management can occur only when the correct consequences are applied immediately and consistently after the target behavior occurs. Correct application is based on two assumptions:

1. Staff attitude. When the target behavior occurs, staff *want* to intervene in a manner consistent with behavioral principles.

2. Staff knowledge and skills. Staff *are able* to intervene correctly and consistently.

Staff Attitude

Most direct care staff and administrators in geriatric facilities are trained to give attention to client needs. Their general philosophy is to increase healthy or appropriate functioning—an approach that is entirely compatible with behavioral philosophy. However, there is often a fundamental difference in the *means* used by behavioral and traditional or medical systems to arrive at this goal. The two systems also differ in their understanding of what constitutes acceptable outcomes of treatments and how these outcomes are measured (see Table 2.1 in Chapter 2).

Without administrative support, behavioral programs applied to an entire unit or ward probably would not be feasible. Individual programs, however, might still be possible. In fact, if programming for a ward is being considered, it may be best to start with individual client programs, including the other residents at a later time. Such individual programs should be selected carefully after thorough evaluation of client cases. The following considerations are important in the early stages of planning any large-scale program:

1. Begin with individuals who are fairly competent and exhibit mild problem behaviors or behaviors that are relatively easy to modify. Early success at the beginning stage is important for its modeling effects and to overcome any initial staff reluctance toward the program.
2. If other staff members need to be involved in data collection or treatment at the beginning stage, try to include only staff who are open to new approaches. Cooperation and a willingness to learn are essential in ensuring the success of a behavioral treatment. Positive reinforcement should be programmed in for the staff, and they should be shown clear evidence of a client's progress during therapy. Use of graphs is particularly effective in this regard.
3. When possible, provide reinforcement and feedback to participating staff members in front of other staff. This approach can help win over other caregivers before any attempt is made to apply the program to the unit or ward.
4. After a few initial successes, try to treat more difficult target behaviors such as wandering or fecal smearing exhibited by more regressed clients. Make sure that baseline data has been taken for some time to demonstrate to staff

the severity of the problem behavior. Include data such as injury reports, linen counts, time the client has spent in isolation, number of prn medications given, and hours of activity attendance.

Hopefully, through these steps the program designer can change both the target behavior and staff attitudes.

Before applying the program on a larger scale, however, the clinician must address the second potential problem—staff knowledge and skills. For programs to succeed, caregivers must learn the principles of behavioral techniques and the skills involved in administering various treatments. Otherwise, behavior therapy techniques have a poor chance of succeeding.

Staff Knowledge and Skills

Changes in attitudes must be matched by acquired knowledge and skills. Before behavior therapy is implemented on a ward or unit, staff should be provided with intensive education and training. Education should continue periodically throughout treatment.

We have used a modular approach in training staff at our facility at the beginning of program implementation. The training package contains six modules covering general behavioral principles, methods for increasing appropriate behavior, and methods for decreasing inappropriate behavior. Staff on behavioral units are required to take all six modules, while other workers may need to learn only selected ones. On the geriatrics unit, two specialized modules have been prepared specifically for employees who must combine knowledge of behavioral techniques with knowledge of elderly clients' characteristic problems. (These modules are presented as Appendices A and B.) Content areas to be covered in staff training are listed in Table 6.1.

Little research has been done on the effects of inservice training on the use of behavioral techniques. However, researchers report that psychiatric nurses have been trained successfully to employ behavioral techniques such as time sampling, extinction, differential reinforcement of other behavior, and satiation (Ayllon & Michael, 1959). Lee and Znachko (1968) report that psychiatric aides were also trained to apply behavior therapy to clients, although the effectiveness of their training has not been validated empirically.

Maintaining Staff Effectiveness

While inservice training is essential in the institutional setting, it is not enough to ensure continued staff compliance with behav-

TABLE 6.1
CONTENT AREAS FOR
INSERVICE TRAINING IN BEHAVIORAL PROGRAMS

Increasing the probability of an adaptive response
Shaping
Gradual approximation
Prompting
Fading
Positive reinforcement
  primary reinforcement
  secondary reinforcement
Principles of immediacy, consistency, and contingency
Token economy
Contracting
Level system

Decreasing the probability of a maladaptive response
Extinction
Time out (from reinforcement)
Seclusion
Differential reinforcement of other behavior (DRO)
Response cost
Restriction
Restitution
Correction
Aversive procedures
  overcorrection
  contingent aversive stimulation
  contingent restraint

Changing the location of a response
Stimulus enhancement
Stimulus control
Selective reinforcement
Discriminative stimulus

ioral techniques. Working with staff-client interactions around daily activities can be even more effective in shaping appropriate client and staff behavior. Periodic modeling on the ward and feedback from supervisors to each staff member are also necessary. It may also be wise to provide periodic training sessions or refresher courses throughout the course of treatment.

Other Problems in Institutional Settings

Many other concerns exist in inpatient facilities that need to be addressed in the early stages of program application. These issues include the inadvertent reinforcement of clients' dependent behavior, delivery of free or noncontingent reinforcement, the need to monitor the side-effects of medication, and the necessity for a reliable data collection system. Since data collection is the backbone of any sound behavioral program, we will address this particular concern first.

The Data System

The importance of a reliable and convenient data system cannot be overstated. It is by far the most essential link in the total behavioral design, for without it interventions are useless. The clinician cannot verify treatment success, determine client progress against goals, pinpoint errors in the treatment program, or even evaluate the program in any meaningful way. The criteria for a data system are as follows:

1. The data collection forms should be easy to read and make recording data simple.
2. The forms should be available to staff at all times so that entries can be made immediately after a target behavior or response has occurred and interventions have been applied.
3. Staff should be able to make entries on the data sheet with as little effort and duplication of other forms of documentation as possible (i.e., progress notes, seclusion/restraint monitoring forms).
4. A transcriber should be able to use information from these forms and present the data in summary (i.e., running tallies, weekly frequency counts, graphs).
5. The forms should have enough space to record all information pertinent to a complete functional analysis for use in designing a specific treatment approach. The information should include a detailed description of the target behavior, the time and location in which the behavior occurs, its duration, the person or object receiving the behavior (if any), the intervention used, and the staff member(s) who intervened or observed the target behavior. Special written cues might also be incorporated on this form to indicate which intervention should be used, the need for a physician's order, and when an incident or injury report may need to be completed.

A sample data recording form is presented in Table 6.2. The form meets the criteria above and has been used successfully in our institution.

TABLE 6.2
SAMPLE DATA RECORDING FORM

Date _____   Ward _____

Client name and time	BEHAVIOR	Physical aggression*	Verbal aggression	Self-injury	Property destruction	Aggressive sexual behavior	Inappropriate smoking	
	INTERVENTION	Room TO	Dorm TO	Response prevention	Room TO	Room TO	Restriction	

Contraband	Stealing	Begging	Spitting	Incontinence	Noncompliance	Other	_Setting_ Victim	Staff
Response cost	Response cost	Extinction	Correction	Correction	Restriction			

*Indicates specifics: H = Hands   F = Foot   Hd = Head   T = Teeth   O = Object   Ot = Other   S = Seclusion ordered

The data from this form are then transcribed onto frequency sheets made out for each client. The frequency information can be translated into curves on a graph to form a profile of each client's target behavior over a number of weeks.

In general, all staff should have access to the behavior recording forms and enter observations and interventions as they occur. However, it may be preferable to assign responsibility for entering data to one staff member each day on each shift. The responsibility can be rotated among shift workers. If the data are to be stored only on paper, the transcriber can be a ward clerk or other designee. A data clerk with computer skills should be employed to enter the information on computer records.

Statement of Problems, Strategies, and Goals

Strategies, problems, and goals for each client should be stated in specific, observable, and measurable terms for two reasons. First, outside review agencies demand such precision and are not satisfied with diagnoses used as problem definitions or with goals that cannot be measured. Second, a client's progress through a program is nearly impossible to measure when the problems are stated ambiguously and the goals are not specific enough so that all staff members can agree on them.

Inappropriate and appropriate care plans are compared in Table 6.3. The differences clearly indicate which plan will lead to more effective treatment design and monitoring.

Monitoring Undesirable Drug Side-Effects

An institution is a good setting in which to observe and monitor drug side-effects. The environment is relatively controlled, and clients are subject to fairly consistent observation. Since drug intake is believed to be known at all times, any undesirable side-effects that appear should be easily traced to a particular medication.

Although a discussion of the pharmacokinetics of medications frequently administered to elderly clients is beyond the scope of this book, we will cover some of the major drug classes and unwanted side-effects that may occur (see also Appendix C). These effects are not idiosyncratic or allergic responses but appear with varying severity and duration in a significant number of elderly clients. In this chapter we include only those drugs that may produce behavioral responses which can affect a target

TABLE 6.3
ENTRIES ON SAMPLE CARE PLANS

Problem	Goals	Approaches
Inappropriate:		
1. Senile dementia	1. Reduce dementia.	1. Medication for confusion and medication for agitation as needed. Observe while ambulating.
	2. Keep comfortable.	2. Provide needs.
Appropriate:		
1. Urinary incontinence	1. Reduce number of accidents to 2 per week.	1. Implement urinary incontinence program.
2. Wandering	2. Reduce wandering by increasing participation in other activities to 50%.	2. Tokens for activity participation.
3. Periodic agitation	3. Reduce frequency of episodes to 1 per week.	3. Minor tranquilizer twice daily or minor tranquilizer as needed.
4. Disorientation to place and time	4. Increase correct orientation responses to 25 on Ward Orientation Scale.	4. Reality Orientation class twice per week. Color cues on doors.

behavior or which may mimic responses that are caused by psychological variables.

Movement disorders such as tremors, facial grimaces, and muscle contractions are among the most frequent and noticeable side-effects. These movements cannot be controlled by clients, although clients may exaggerate the movements when they are upset or need to gain attention. Movement disorders generally fall into three classes: extrapyramidal, tardive dyskinesia, and dystonia.

1. Extrapyramidal. These side-effects include various muscle tremors similar to those of Parkinson's disease, motor restlessness, and a compulsive pill-rolling motion of the forefinger and thumb.

2. Tardive dyskinesia. This disorder involves the oral-buccal-lingual area of the face and appears as lip smacking, tongue thrusting or darting, tongue tremors, or puckering.
3. Dystonia. This side-effect manifests as muscle contraction-release cycles involving the neck, upper torso, or pelvis.

The extent to which these problems interfere with clients' daily functioning depends on the severity and duration of the side-effects. For example, tremors can make eating or drinking difficult, while tongue thrusting can reduce the amount of food a client actually swallows.

Movement disorders can be spotted fairly easily once they are full blown. Early detection, however, may be more difficult. For example, tardive dyskinesia mimics the actions of someone adjusting loose dentures or chewing food. The problem may go unnoticed until the behavior worsens. So far, no adequate treatment for tardive dyskinesia has been found. It can be temporarily masked by increasing the dosage of the medication that produced the side-effect.

These movement disorders are caused primarily by the major tranquilizing drugs. As a result, the presence of more than one neuroleptic in a client's medical history, particularly over time, should alert the clinician to watch for any type of movement disorder. For a more quantitative measure of these disorders, time sampling may be used (Hussian, Hill, & Ward, 1982). Exhibit 6.1, following this chapter, provides a sample checklist for listing drug side-effects.

Other drug side-effects that may mimic behavioral disorders include lethargy, impotence, confusion, insomnia, hallucinations, irritability, delirium, nightmares, and anxiety. Table 6.4 lists the more frequently prescribed medications that can cause these behavioral side-effects. Whenever these responses develop rapidly in clients and correlate with starting one or more of these medications, the observer should suspect the drug as a source of the problem and alert the physician.

CASE STUDY #6
A 66-year-old female, with no history of mental illness, was admitted to a long-term care facility for multiple physical problems. These included diabetes mellitus,

TABLE 6.4
COMMONLY PRESCRIBED DRUGS AND
BEHAVIORAL SIDE-EFFECTS

Drug	*Behavioral side-effects*
Amantadine (Symmetrel)	Hallucinations
Anticonvulsants	Hallucinations, delirium, confusion, lethargy, depression
Antidepressants	Atropine psychosis, sedation, agitation
Antihistamines	Delirium, sedation
Atropine	Confusion, delirium, mania, hallucinations, disorientation
Benztropine (Cogentin)	See atropine
Cimetidine (Tagamet)	Confusion, delirium, disorientation, hallucinations
Corticosteroids	Depression, mania, hallucinations
Diazepam (Valium) and related compounds	Excitement, hallucinations, depression
Digitalis	Confusion, paranoia, amnesia
Doxepin (Sinequan)	See atropine
Indomethacin (Indocin)	Confusion, paranoia, depression, hallucinations
Levodopa	Delirium, agitation, mania
Lidocaine (Xylocaine)	Confusion
Methyldopa (Aldomet)	Depression, hallucinations
Methylphenidate (Ritalin)	Hallucinations
Pentazocine (Talwin)	Hallucinations, disorientation, panic, confusion
Phenobarbital	Hyperactivity, depression
Phenylephrine (Neo-Synephrine)	Depression, hallucinations
Propranolol (Inderal)	Depression, confusion, hallucinations, paranoia
Rauwolfia alkaloids	Depression
Tricyclic antidepressants	See atropine

Note: Also see Appendix C, Drug Education Program.

cataracts, and hypertension. She had been at the facility for approximately 6 months and was quite active in the programs and involved with other residents.

The physician in the care facility prescribed an antihypertensive and a diuretic to control the rather labile hypertension. Nursing staff noticed that within weeks of taking the medication, the client became withdrawn, tearful, and confined herself to bed. This behavior was in striking contrast to her previous level of participation in activities and social interaction.

The physician ordered tests to determine if a physical cause was at the root of the client's problem. It was found that her potassium level was 2.1 mEq/L, somewhat below the normal range. He prescribed a potassium supplement. Within 1 week, the client was returning to her previous rate of participation. Her emotional responses were more appropriate, and she reported feeling less fatigued and more interested in her surroundings. A follow-up test revealed her potassium level to be 4.2 mEq/L.

This case illustrates the importance of testing for side-effects to medication and for a physical cause of abrupt and drastic changes in behavior. Had the client's responses been treated as evidence of senile dementia or some other emotional disorder of aging, she would not have received the proper treatment.

When a client on any of the medications listed in Table 6.4 is discharged from an institution, the client and family members or caregivers should be told to watch for side-effects. The mental health professional should be careful not to alarm the client and others unduly. Side-effects do not always occur or, when they do, may not always mean the drug must be discontinued. The client and caregivers should simply be aware of the possible adverse reactions so they can inform the physician when such disorders occur. This educational procedure usually increases the likelihood that clients will continue to take their medication. A sample drug education program is provided in Appendix C. The program can be copied or adapted and presented to the client or the client's principal caregiver(s) at discharge.

Assessing Mental Status and Other Functions

The initial intake in a geriatric institution can be conducted in many ways. It may well be the most important step in providing clients with appropriate care and treatment. As a result, the procedure, regardless of format, should cover not only orientation but also affective considerations, memory capacity, and overt manifestations of underlying problems (e.g., drug side-effects, soft neurological signs, asymmetries, and the like).

Although different agencies may have different requirements for the content of initial assessments, the following elements should be included:

1. A short mental status examination should be conducted to reveal the client's memory for personal data, recent major events, and immediate events such as date and season. (A sample assessment form is presented as Exhibit 3.2 at the end of Chapter 3.) If the client makes any gross mistakes on these questions, the clinician should look for signs of dementia or delirium. Answers which are irrelevant to the questions might suggest schizophrenic processes. Replies such as "I don't know" or "It doesn't matter" may indicate depression.

2. A measure of affect should be made that is more objective than most assessments. An example of such an instrument is included as Exhibit 6.2, following this chapter.

3. The client's concentration, memory, and speech processes should be assessed to distinguish between a dementia etiology and other disorders. An extremely short attention span, poor recent and long-term memory, and speech that disintegrates shortly after initiation can be indicators of a dementing illness. Exhibit 6.3 provides a sample rating scale designed for this type of assessment.

4. Shortly after admission, the clinician should assess the client's level of functioning on the ward in a variety of skill areas. The presence or absence of these skills can determine alternative placement and the likelihood of discharge to a referral setting. Toileting, dressing, ambulation, feeding, socialization, and medication compliance should be assessed in this regard. Exhibit 6.4 presents a sample adaptive functioning scale.

5. The degree of orientation should be addressed during the initial evaluation and periodically throughout the client's stay. Though the geriatric assessment form (Exhibit 3.2) includes questions designed to evaluate the client's degree of orientation, a more specific and complete scale is helpful.

   It is also better to include a measure of orientation that has some functional use. That is, instead of the more traditional measures that cover orientation to time, place, person, and recent events, attempts should be made to measure a client's response to ward cues. These cues are essential, since they help clients find their way around the ward; locate rooms, toilets, dining areas, and other places; avoid dangerous areas; and learn the rules and guidelines for behavior. Failure to respond to these cues can indicate profound disabilities and an inability to learn new response-cue associations. Exhibit 6.5 provides a sample quantitative scale to measure ward orientation on admission and periodically throughout the client's stay. Point totals can be used to monitor a client's progress throughout the program or the results of therapeutic interventions.

6. Activity level should be measured, particularly when the presenting problem includes depression. A major goal of treatment within an institutional setting is to increase clients' activity levels and their access to stimulation. As a result, the clinician must have some way to measure change in these functional areas. The best measure is time sampling of actual participation in activities, social interaction, and the like (a sample time-sampling form is presented as Exhibit 3.1 in Chapter 3). While observation periods can vary, 15 minutes is usually a suitable interval for observing and documenting these behaviors.

7. A measure of drug side-effects should be made on admission and periodically throughout the resident's stay. Monitoring side-effects is particularly important when a new medication is prescribed or a current one increased. (See Exhibit 6.1, Table 6.4, and Appendix C for a list of side-effects of commonly prescribed drugs.)

8. A complete physical examination should be conducted by the admitting physician. The exam should emphasize physical findings and any facts in a client's medical history that may have a bearing on current abnormal behavior. Medical personnel should conduct a variety of tests routinely upon admission and select additional tests if necessary. The results of these examinations can determine whether physical problems such as thyroidism, an electrolyte imbalance, anemia, pulmonary insufficiency, fractures, or impactions are causing psychological disturbances. A list of diagnostic tests is presented in Table 6.5, while laboratory values are provided in Exhibit 6.6, following this chapter. Please note that these ranges are derived from a younger client sample.

TABLE 6.5
DIAGNOSTIC TESTS TO AID
DIFFERENTIAL ASSESSMENT

*Electrolytes	EEG
Renal function test	Neuropsychological battery
*Complete blood count (CBC)	CT scan
Thyroid function test	X-ray of other areas
Syphilis screen (VDRL)	Rectal exam for impaction
*Chest X-ray	*General physical
EKG	

*Routine

Problems of Noncontingent Reinforcement

Noncontingent or free reinforcement is a major problem in institutions using behavior management programs. Staff, family, and other visitors may provide clients with reinforcers that are not contingent upon targeted appropriate behavior or that may actually reinforce inappropriate behavior. The problem occurs usually because the individuals are not aware of the behavioral program or because they do not have sufficient interest in the client's condition.

Noncontingent reinforcement may be the most frequent program error that the clinician encounters. It generally takes one of the following forms:

1. Giving the client cigarettes or other reinforcers for performing work that is ordinarily a staff member's responsibility.
2. Giving the client cigarettes or other reinforcers to calm the person or to avoid a possible escalation of verbal or physical aggression.
3. Providing positive reinforcement in response to the client's begging for these items or for persistent requests for attention.
4. Providing positive reinforcement for only a limited performance of the targeted behavior.

These reinforcing behaviors on the part of staff are difficult to discover. Once observed, the behavior should be stopped quickly and consequences administered, ranging from counseling or education about the program to restrictions on career advancement.

CASE STUDY #7

A 69-year-old male, a long-term resident of a geriatric unit in a state mental institution, had several behaviors targeted for change by his treatment team. The behaviors included withdrawal, a low level of activity, physical aggression, thought disorder, and periodic self-abuse.

The client was receiving a neuroleptic and earned tokens for participating in therapies and classes. During a 1-month span, the client regressed significantly and refused to take part in activities. He no longer earned enough tokens to receive his favorite items from the token store.

A functional analysis of the client's behavior failed to reveal the cause of his regression and exacerbation of his psychosis. Then it was accidentally discovered that one of the staff members was taking the client off the ward during his break in the late afternoon. The client and employee were observed in the vending machine area where the client was given coffee and snacks and ate with the staff member.

In essence, the client was receiving free reinforcement without being required to show any level of acceptable, independent response to earn the reinforcers. The staff member was either unaware of the treatment program for this client or unwilling to abide by its restrictions. Naturally, the client chose the "cost-free" reinforcement.

When the staff member was reminded of the treatment program, he stopped taking the client with him on breaks. Without the free reinforcement, the client began earning tokens at his previous rate, and his activity and participation levels increased.

This case points out the importance of all staff members adhering to treatment guidelines and requirements. If clients are given additional "free" reinforcement, they will have less incentive to participate in the treatment program or change their behavior.

The problem of staff providing noncontingent reinforcement can be largely avoided by taking several steps.

1. Monitor staff-client interactions throughout the program.
2. Assign behavioral program units to employees who accept and support behavioral technology.
3. Show staff, through example, how to provide appropriate intervention.
4. Demonstrate the outcome of interventions correctly applied.

Such steps can help clinicians gain staff support for their programs and prevent noncontingent reinforcement from being provided either inadvertently or through misunderstanding of program goals and objectives. In our experience, using threats and punishment to change staff or family attitudes rarely if ever achieves the desired goal.

Maintaining Dependent Behavior

Unfortunately, institutional settings are ripe for staff members to maintain clients' dependent behavior. Clients are not encouraged to do things for themselves or expand their abilities to function independently. Dependent behavior has been defined by Baltes and others as responses that promote condescension from and care provision by others (Baltes, Burgess, & Stewart, 1980; Barton, Baltes, & Orzech, 1980). This type of behavior appears to be supported by staff members for several reasons:

1. High staff-to-client ratios mean that staff members do not have time to give each client proper reinforcement for appropriate, adaptive, and independent behavior. On the contrary, most staff attention is focused on clients who are acting inappropriately and who are disruptive or persistent in their demands for attention.
2. The staff may be afraid of legal consequences if they ignore any requests for assistance or medication. Well-publicized malpractice and negligence lawsuits tend to make staff respond to client requests rather than attempt to shape behavior or promote self-care or coping strategems.
3. Most of the training that direct care workers receive in nursing, medicine, and rehabilitation fields encourages reinforcing clients when a dependent act occurs. If a client appears to be in pain, unable to dress, or suffering from depression, staff are trained to supply whatever is needed to take care of the problem immediately.

4. It takes less time, in the short run, to provide a requested item or service than to wait for the client to attempt some independent action and then reinforce it. Prompting and shaping procedures usually do require more time than simply giving a client the requested service or medical attention but in fact they can be more time saving in the long run.

Studies have shown that supporting dependent behavior in clients can also encourage residents to become more dependent the longer they are in the facility. Baltes, Honn, Barton, Orzech, and Lago (1983) reported that staff in nursing homes tended to follow both dependent and independent client behavior with dependency-supportive behavior of their own. Mean age of residents was 81.2 years. For example, only 4% of the clients' independent self-care behavior was reinforced while 37% of the independent behavior was followed by inadvertent extinction.

Thus, we can view clients' dependent behavior as partly a function of the staff's dependency-supportive responses. This approach suggests possible behavioral techniques to change staff attitudes and actions.

1. Show staff members the difference between the dependent and independent behaviors that clients are likely to exhibit. Dependent behavior would include asking for assistance, having the food tray delivered to the table, refusing to feed themselves, and responding only to physical prompts and not verbal ones. Independent behavior includes independent ambulation, locating and using ash trays, cleaning their beds and locker areas, and requiring no prompting for grooming and self-care.
2. Make staff aware of their responses when clients exhibit dependent and independent behaviors. Some of these actions are listed in Table 6.6. Clinicians should discuss these and similar responses observed in staff-client interactions on the ward or unit.
3. Teach staff members behavioral shaping procedures.
4. Point out those clients who have been determined through treatment program and/or physical examinations to be physically incapable of performing certain types of independent behaviors. It may be that these clients can be taught or retaught part of an independent behavior—such

TABLE 6.6
STAFF STATEMENTS SUPPORTING
DEPENDENT VERSUS INDEPENDENT BEHAVIORS

Dependency supportive	*Independency supportive*
Ambulation	
1. Here, let me help you to the dining room.	1. You can make it fine if you start a little sooner.
2. Better get in the wheel chair and I'll push you to the clinic.	2. If you can walk to the canteen, you can walk to the clinic.
Grooming	
1. I'll brush it for you. You're doing it all wrong.	1. Keep trying. It looks better.
2. Don't worry about the way you look. Your family won't be here until next week.	2. Put some makeup on if it makes you feel better.
3. I'll change you. You're wet.	3. Change your pants and clean up this area here.
Activity	
1. Let her stay in bed. She gets fussy when we try to get her up.	1. Prompt her out of bed. The activity is about to start.
2. You're pretty old. You'd better rest.	2. An hour nap is enough for someone as fit as you.
3. Why do you want a job assignment? You're not going anywhere.	3. Fill out an application if you wish.
Feeding	
1. I'll feed you. We're running late.	1. You need to get here earlier so that you can feed yourself at your own pace.
2. You're making such a mess. Let me help.	2. You can wash up later. You are eating better.

as getting to the dining room on their own even though they may not be able to handle a knife and fork. Or they may not be able to undress themselves, turn on the shower, or bathe completely without assistance, but they may be able to wash smaller areas or pat certain parts of themselves dry. These smaller responses of a larger behavior should be targeted for reinforcement and shaping.

Transition to Less Restrictive Settings

In any behavior therapy program, it is important to include factors that will help the client make the transition to a less restrictive setting. It is one thing to shape, reduce, or increase behaviors that are appropriate on a closed ward. It is quite another to consider what behavioral cues or reinforcement will be necessary once the current treatment program is over. To design a program otherwise is to do clients a considerable disservice.

A transition program should seek to accomplish two goals. First, it should gradually make the contingencies provided resemble those given in the less restrictive setting. Second, it should require the type and level of response from clients that are likely to be positively reinforced in that setting. In other words, clinicians must require more independent and higher levels of functioning from clients than would be expected of them in a more restrictive institution. The transition can be encouraged in several different ways.

1. For clients who will be transferred to their homes or to halfway houses, token systems can be faded and contracts used to increase appropriate behaviors. The token system, while often necessary when first building adaptive response rates, is more artificial than contingencies found in less restrictive settings. In such settings, verbal and written contracts are more likely to be used.

2. For clients functioning at lower levels, training stimuli from the institution can be used in the home, nursing home, or other facility. Stimuli used in stimulus control or enhancement techniques can be placed in corresponding locations in the new setting.

3. Whenever possible, the clinician should bring the client's family into the care planning and provision process before discharging the client. Family members should be taught to prompt and reinforce appropriate behaviors and should have the chance to "practice" under the guidance of the mental health professional. This approach not only helps educate family members, but may also help the client generalize treatment through the use of several "therapists."

4. Whenever possible, permit clients to visit the nursing home or other alternative setting to overcome their fear of the unknown. At the least, show clients pictures of the new facility, both the outside and interior.

5. Transition groups for clients who are to be discharged in the near future allow clients to discuss their fears and expectations and try out problem-solving techniques introduced by the clinician or other caregivers. These groups can also be used to discuss issues such as family conflicts that may hinder transition, concerns about taking medication properly, ways to use the services available in the new setting, and methods of coping with new demands that may be made on them in the new residence.

6. Specific discharge programs can be sent with the client to the new residence or to the home. In addition to the drug education program (Appendix C), discharge programs covering behaviors like wandering (Appendix D), agitation and combativeness (Appendix E), and inappropriate sexual behavior (Appendix F) should be sent with the client's discharge papers. The programs are particularly useful for direct care personnel in nursing and rest homes, and they should reduce the likelihood that clients will be returned when exhibiting a mild management problem.

Special considerations and problems for the caregiver are likely to arise when clients are discharged to the home or are referred from a home environment. The next chapter presents guidelines for handling these problems and for working with this particular client population.

EXHIBIT 6.1
DRUG SIDE-EFFECTS CHECKLIST

Client

Date

Ward

Staff

	Yes	No	Comments*
1. Extrapyramidal side-effects			
Fine tremors of the hands			
Constant pacing			
Constant leg crossing			
Up-and-down in seat			
Rubbing, patting, fidgeting			
Pill rolling of thumb and forefinger			
2. Tardive dyskinesia			
Tremors of the tongue			
Tongue flicking, less than 1.0 cm			
Tongue thrusting, more than 1.0 cm			
Lip smacking or puckering			
3. Dystonia			
Neck contraction-relaxations			
Upper torso thrusting			
Pelvic thrusting			
4. Autonomic side-effects			
Urinary retention			
Dry mouth			
Blurred or impaired vision			
5. Other side-effects			
Increased photosensitivity			
Strange pigmentation			
Increased lens opacity			
6. Signs of toxicity			
Slurred speech			
Staggered gait			
Falling			
Hypotension (orthostatic)			
Lethargy or daytime sleepiness			

*Also for time-sampling data

EXHIBIT 6.2
ASSESSMENT OF AFFECTIVE STATES

Client _____   Date _____

Ward _____   Observer _____

Anxious

1. Short attention span
2. Increased fine motor movements
3. Increased gross motor movements
4. Easy distractability
5. Tense posturing
6. Somatic complaints _____
7. Sweating
8. Increased pulse rate _____
9. Muscle tics
10. Poor eye fixation
11. Reported anxiety
12. Avoidance behavior
13. Phobic behavior
14. History of anxiety
15. High number of stressors
16. Target physical conditions
17. Target medications
18. Sleep disturbance
19. Other _____
_____

Depressed

1. Slow verbal response
2. Slow motor response
3. Low speech production
4. Low motor production
5. Memory deficits
6. Poor appetite
7. Sleep disturbance
8. Lack of spontaneity
9. Monotonic speech
10. Poor eye fixation
11. Head down or body slump
12. Reported depression or sadness
13. History of depression
14. Suicidal verbalizations
15. Hopelessness
16. Helplessness
17. Fatigue, tiredness
18. Somatic complaints _____
19. Non-participation
20. Recent losses
21. Anti-hypertensive drugs
22. Target physical conditions
23. Low sensory thresholds
24. Other _____
_____

Target medications _____
Target physical conditions _____
Comments and specifications* _____
_____

*Includes the results of time sampling

117

EXHIBIT 6.3
BRIEF COGNITIVE RATING SCALE

Client	Date

Ward	Staff

Axis	*Rating (Circle highest score)*
	1 No evidence of a deficit in concentration.
	2 Poor concentration (Serial 7's from 100).
1	3 Very poor concentration (4's from 100).
Concentration	4 Extreme deficit (2's from 20).
	5 Forgets the task. Counts forward.
	6 Cannot count forward to 10 by 1's.
	1 No evidence of a deficit.
	2 Complains of forgetting names more now than before.
2	3 Deficit with specific but not major events.
Recent memory	4 Deficit with major events.
	5 Unsure of current date.
	6 Spotty knowledge of some recent events.
	7 No knowledge of recent events.
	1 No impairment in past memory.
	2 Some gaps with probing.
3	3 Knows children, job; not school or homes.
Past memory	4 Knows job; not number or names of children.
	5 No memory of past with confabulation.
	6 No memory of past without confabulation.
	1 Rational, fluent, and spontaneous.
	2 Rational, labored, and hesitant.
	3 Rational, slurred.
4	4 Rational, some word search difficulty.
Speech	5 Begins rationally, then disintegrates.
	6 Disintegrates, uses nonexistent words.
	7 Completely irrelevant.
	8 Mutism or echolalia.

EXHIBIT 6.4
LEVEL OF ADAPTIVE FUNCTIONING

Client   Date

Ward   Staff

1. *Toileting*

   Prior to voiding or evacuation, how far does the patient get before actual elimination?

   a. No apparent recognition of need to toilet.

   b. Minimal body movement (e.g., attempts to stand) immediately prior to elimination.

   c. Indicates need to toilet but with insufficient time to take to toilet.

   d. Indicates need to toilet with sufficient time.

   e. Walks/propels to rest room, but begins elimination prior to reaching receptacle.

   f. Reaches receptacle but does not bare self.

   g. Bares self appropriately.

2. *Dressing*

   What is the least amount of assistance involved in the process of dressing this patient?

   a. Not capable of participating in dressing procedure.

   b. Requires physical prompting.

   c. Requires verbal prompting for each article of clothing.

   d. Requires only an initial prompt.

   e. Initiates dressing without any prompting.

3. *Ambulation*

   Which of the following describes the patient's ambulation ability best?

   a. Confined to wheel chair or bed.

   b. Ambulation severely restricted due to feeble gait.

   c. Ambulation with assistance of two parties only.

   d. Ambulation with assistance of one party only.

   e. Ambulation with light guidance or environmental prop only.

   f. Ambulation alone with careful monitoring.

   g. Ambulation alone with minimal monitoring.

EXHIBIT 6.4 *(continued)*

4. *Feeding*

Which of the following describes the patient's feeding best?

   a. Unable to feed self with any food items.

   b. Able to feed self but not able to use utensils alone.

   c. Utensil loaded and brought to mouth with continual physical guidance.

   d. Utensil loaded with help but brought to mouth without assistance.

   e. Utensil loaded and brought to mouth without assistance but with significant spillage.

   f. Utensil loaded and brought to mouth without assistance without spillage.

5. *Socialization*

Which of the following describes the patient's social interactions best?

   a. Remains in solitary area with no interactions.

   b. Remains in solitary area except for dining.

   c. Sits in common areas with no social interaction.

   d. Sits in common areas with interaction only when initiated by others.

   e. Participates in on-ward activities with prompting.

   f. Participates in on-ward activities without prompting.

   g. Initiates on-ward activities and interactions of an appropriate nature.

6. *Medication consumption*

   a. Frequent (at least once per day) refusal to take medication.

   b. Some (at least twice weekly) refusal to take medication.

   c. Takes medication readily but not capable of self-medication.

   d. Shows some ability to self-medicate but unreliable and requires observation.

   e. Shows ability to self-medicate but will require periodic laboratory checks.

   f. Shows ability to self-medicate.

   g. Ability to self-medicate not evaluated.

EXHIBIT 6.5
PATIENT ORIENTATION SCALE

Client	Date

Ward	Staff

1. *Ward*

   (Start with patient at door of nurse's station and proceed in order down list.)

a. Locates designated bay area	1	0
b. Locates bed	1	0
c. Locates locker	1	0
d. Locates nursing station	1	0
e. Locates bathroom	1	0
f. Locates medication room	1	0
g. Locates dining exit	1	0
h. Locates bathing room	1	0
i. Locates token store	1	0
(If store is not located on patient's ward, simple directions will suffice, e.g., "downstairs.")		
j. Locates patio area	1	0

   Total

2. *Personnel*

   (Since professionals a-d are not always on the ward, pictures should be provided for the patient to identify. A correct matching of picture with profession is all that is required for a successful score. Since members of remaining positions are frequently available, simply pointing out the appropriate person is sufficient.)

a. Nurse	1	0
b. Physician	1	0
c. Social worker	1	0
d. Psychologist	1	0
e. Aides	1	0
f. Rehabilitation workers (activity leader)	1	0
g. Other patients	1	0
(Patient must give the first or last name of another patient.)		

   Total

EXHIBIT 6.5 *(continued)*

3. *External information*
   a. Full name   1   0
   b. Day and date   1   0
   (Answering one is sufficient.)
   c. Month and year   1   0
   d. Place   1   0
   e. Last meal eaten   1   0
   f. President   1   0
   g. Previous president   1   0
   h. Season of year   1   0

                                                            Total ____

4. *Personal information*
   a. Lists immediate family members (parents, spouse,   1   0
   children) and their status— living or deceased
   b. Knows birthdate (month, date, year) and place of birth   1   0
   c. Aware of financial assets (e.g., Social Security monthly   1   0
   income; major possessions such as houses, land, etc.; net
   worth. No major omissions or additions will be sufficient.)
   d. Aware of reason for admission   1   0
   e. Aware of problems that are being treated   1   0
   f. Aware of medication (When presented with medications,   1   0
   patient can give brief statement as to their purpose,
   e.g., nerves, depression, dosage quantity, and time of
   day they are taken.)
   g. Aware of therapy programs patient is involved in   1   0
   h. Aware of personal possessions at hospital (Check   1   0
   personal effects and clothing record.)
   i. Aware of level (II, III, IV of behavior level system)   1   0
   j. Aware of length of stay (within 1 week if here $<$ 6 weeks,   1   0
   within 3 weeks if here $>$ 6 weeks but $<$ 6 months; within
   1 month if here $>$ 6 months but $<$ 3 years; within 1 year
   if here $>$ 3 years)

                                                            Total ____

                                                      Grand Total ____

We would like to thank D. Nicholson for his design of this form.

EXHIBIT 6.6
LABORATORY NORMALS

Test	Normal range
BUN	6–21 MG/DL
Calcium	9.0–11.0 mg/dl
Carbamazepine (Tegretol)	4.0–12.0 ug/ml
Chloride	96–106 mEq/L
Creatinine	0.4–1.5 MG/DL
Digoxin	0.8–3.0 ng/dl
Dilantin	10–20 UG/ML
Fasting blood sugar	70–110 mg/dl
Hematocrit	
Male	47 ± 5%
Female	42 ± 5%
Hemoglobin	
Male	16 ± 2 g/dl
Female	14 ± 2 g/dl
Lithium	0.6–1.2 mEq/L
Phenobarbital	10–40 UG/ML
Potassium	3.5–5.0 mEq/L
Primidone (Mysoline)	5.0–15.0 UG/ML
SGOT	0–22 units
Sodium	135–148 mEq/L
T3	33–45%
T4	5.5–11.5 ug/dl
TSH	1.9–5.4 IU/ML
FTI	2.2–4.7 units
Uric Acid	2.5–8.0 MG/DL

Note: Age-adjusted laboratory ranges are not currently available. The upper and lower limits of some values will be extended for the elderly.

7

Outpatient and Family Considerations

Families of elderly impaired patients often face many difficult choices and decisions in providing proper care for their relatives. As a result, family members may contact a mental health professional when problems or sensitive issues arise. These issues usually include effective methods of home management, family members' stress in coping with the elderly relative, a need to understand the elderly person's behavior, and help in placing the patient in a nursing home or similar facility when home care is no longer possible.

The clinician must be prepared to help these families evaluate their situation and make decisions in the best interests of all concerned. In this chapter, we discuss the major issues that clinicians are likely to encounter in consulting with families of the elderly impaired.

Behavior Management in the Home

Our suggestions for handling behavior problems of elderly impaired patients are similar to those of Haley (1983). His approach involves teaching assessment and behavior management skills to the family of the elderly impaired person. The therapist supervises the family's implementation of the behavioral program. These techniques should adhere to established methods of behavioral assessment and management. As illustrated in Chapter 6, many behavioral methods can be learned and used by nonprofessionals. Caretakers of elderly impaired clients who are taught behavior management skills and then apply them in the home care setting have had success in treating behavioral deficits and excesses such as self-care, incontinence, self-feeding, hygiene, and ambulation (Pinkston & Linsk, 1984). Therefore, family members, as well as aides and other supportive staff, can be trained to apply behavioral techniques and to monitor change.

The following guidelines may be helpful for the clinician working with family members to design a home behavior management program.

1. Make a realistic assessment of the elderly relative's capabilities and limitations. For example, families should not expect a complete restoration of continence in a patient who is in the latter stages of Alzheimer's disease. The clinician should stress that behavioral interventions can often help improve skills and sometimes slow down degeneration of abilities. The interventions may not, however, correct some targeted behaviors completely.

2. Assess family conflicts that may be maintaining or exacerbating a behavior problem or that may interfere with effective intervention. If one spouse, for instance, focuses on the elderly relative's problems to avoid facing issues in the marriage, a behavioral intervention targeting the elderly relative's behavior is not likely to be successful.

3. Select one problem behavior at a time for intervention. If possible, choose a problem that can be treated easily to provide reinforcement for the family's efforts. They are more likely then to maintain their intervention when treating difficult problem behaviors.

4. Define the selected problem behavior in specific, observable terms. Family members frequently will complain that their relative is easily agitated or upset. The clinician must ask detailed questions to determine the exact behavior observed, the conditions under which it occurs, how often it happens, and the consequences that follow.

Such questioning can be integrated with instruction in behavioral principles. For example, the clinician, during an interview with the caretaker of an elderly impaired relative, may find that the caretaker receives numerous phone calls from the relative throughout the day. Each time the relative calls, the caretaker talks with him or her for 10 to 15 minutes trying to convince the relative to limit the number of phone calls. At this point, the clinician may discuss the possibility that talking to the relative about limiting the phone calls may actually be reinforcing the calls. This analysis can then lead to instruction on the principle of reinforcement and how it applies in this particular case.

5. Have family members record a baseline detailing the frequency and/or duration of the behavior, the context, and their management approach. This information will enable the clinician to determine what inappropriate interventions may be aggravating the problem behavior, the setting variables implicated in its maintenance, and a record of frequency and/or duration that can be used for comparison to gauge a program's effectiveness.

6. After presenting the treatment plan, the clinician should determine how well the family members understand the procedure. Have them explain the steps involved in the treatment, rehearse the techniques to be used, and ask any questions or clear up any points they may not understand. For behavioral techniques to be successful, the family should have some knowledge of the underlying principles and how they are applied to problem(s) presented by the family.

7. During the first few days the behavioral interventions are implemented, the clinician should check frequently with family members to provide support and to determine if the plan is being applied correctly. This is the time to make changes in the program to ensure its effectiveness.

The specific techniques outlined in previous chapters for use in institutional settings also can be applied in home management with minor modifications. We discuss these modifications below, along with some general considerations for home behavior management that may be unique to the home setting.

1. Simplify the environment. The elderly demented person is more likely to become confused and unable to locate needed articles in a cluttered room. Remove as many distracting stimuli as possible.

2. To aid in maintaining stimulus control, minimize changes in the environment. Do not rearrange furniture frequently, place toilet articles or clothing in different locations, and the like. The patient is likely to be less upset by lapses of memory if items used frequently are kept in plain sight on top of a bureau or bedside table. Make sure each item has a place where it is always kept.

3. Provide a dependable, structured routine and vary it as little as possible. For example, deliver meals at the same time

each day, perform grooming and other personal care services at a set time, schedule favorite activities so the patient knows when they will occur, and the like.

4. Simplify tasks to encourage independent behavior. If the patient has a problem with fine motor skills, provide clothing without buttons or snaps and substitute loafers for tie shoes. Eating can be simplified by providing sandwiches and other foods the patient can pick up with the hands instead of using utensils. If the patient can manipulate silverware, prepare foods beforehand to minimize the need to cut, pry apart, and the like.

5. Use memory prompts and stimulus enhancement. Have a clock and calendar in plain view to help the patient keep track of the time and day of the month. Also, brief notes may be helpful as memory aids. For example, an elderly woman frequently became upset because she could not remember if her social security check had been deposited. Her daughter wrote a note with the date of deposit and put it in her purse. Whenever the woman looked in her handbag, she saw the note and knew that the check was safely in the bank. Also, dresser drawers can be labeled with color-coded pictures indicating their contents.

6. Be sure the elderly person gets adequate exercise. Regular exercise can improve appetite and sleeping habits and help decrease wandering behavior. A short walk each day or some other regular physical activity the person enjoys can help maintain general health.

Behavior Problems in the Home

Many of the behavior problems exhibited in a nursing home or other facility may also occur in the home. In this section we offer some additional suggestions to help family members manage problem behaviors in the elderly relative. For a more detailed account of practical interventions that family members can use with the elderly demented person, see Mace and Rabins' *The 36-Hour Day* (1981) or Powell and Courtice's *Alzheimer's Disease: A Guide for Families* (1983). These books are written especially for the lay public.

Incontinence

Family members should offer the toilet at regular intervals throughout the day—usually every 2 to 3 hours. A watch or alarm clock can be set for the times that toileting is to be offered. Receptacles that the elderly person might mistake for a toilet (wastebaskets, boxes) should be covered or removed. Open containers should be placed well away from the toilet. If night bed-wetting is a problem, it may help to limit the intake of fluids in the evening and offer the toilet before the person retires. A plastic bed pad may need to be placed over the mattress as well. If incontinence continues despite all these measures, disposable adult diapers can be used. However, the family caretaker should watch closely for skin irritations that may appear. If frequent incontinence is a problem, a physician should be consulted to determine if medical disorders such as a urinary tract infection are the cause.

Sleep Disturbance/Nocturnal Wandering

The demented elderly person often experiences trouble sleeping or may awaken in the dark and become confused and disoriented. A night light may prevent such confusion and can be installed easily. Insomnia or broken sleep can be alleviated by minimizing distracting sounds or bright lights that may shine through the windows. Exercise during the day and limiting daytime napping may also help the patient sleep more soundly. If these techniques do not work, the family caretaker should consult a physician about the use of sleeping aids, including medications. (See also Appendix D.)

Agitated Behavior

At times elderly people with mental or physical disabilities become frustrated at their inability to complete tasks they once performed easily. Or they may become upset at a family member's prompting. When such occasions arise, the family caretaker should not become angry in return and attempt to force or restrain the elderly person. Such action will only make the situation worse. Instead, the family member should use the techniques of distraction and redirection, taking advantage of the elderly person's short memory span. In many cases, the relative can be distracted until the original incident that sparked the emotional flareup is forgotten. (See also Appendix E.)

Dangerous Behavior

The elderly relative may attempt to perform tasks that previously presented no problem but that now may be dangerous because of the individual's memory and judgment deficits. For example, the person may leave food to burn on the stove or mix ingredients that could start a fire. In other cases, the elderly relative may overdose on medication, take medication prescribed for other family members, or mistakenly drink household cleanser thinking it is water.

The family caretaker should make sure that cabinets containing dangerous chemicals or medications are securely fastened with safety latches. Electrical appliances should be stored out of reach or have an additional switch installed that must be tripped before the appliance can be turned on. The house must be safety-proofed as if for a small child, and the family caretaker should be constantly vigilant to guard against accidents.

Hygiene Problems

Often there is no easy solution when the elderly impaired relative balks at prompts to bathe, shave, use a toothbrush, and perform other self-care tasks. However, the family member can lessen potential problems by reproducing the person's prior hygiene routine as closely as possible. If the person always rose at 6:00 a.m., toileted, bathed, and shaved before eating breakfast, this routine should be continued if possible. Also, the individual should be allowed to perform these tasks as independently as possible, within safety and physical constraints. When prompting is needed, the caretaker should use verbal prompts first before attempting manual guidance. If the elderly relative becomes upset at the prompting, it should be stopped temporarily and the person distracted until the emotional reaction fades.

When the elderly person bathes, be sure the water is tepid. Never let the individual adjust the temperature alone since many older people lose their sensitivity to temperature extremes and may get the water too hot or too cold.

Substitute an electric shaver for a razor. The shaver is easier for the elderly person to use independently without the risk of nicks and cuts and does not involve lathering the face with shaving cream. By simplifying routine tasks, the family caretaker can increase the chance that the elderly person will continue to perform them as independently as possible.

Caretaker Stress

Caring for an elderly impaired relative can put considerable stress on family members, particularly the primary caregiver(s). The constant vigilance and frequent prompting and care can be exhausting and create various stress-related problems. The family member is "trapped" in the situation 24 hours a day and has no opportunity to take time off as do personnel in a nursing home.

The clinician can offer several ways for the family caretaker to cope with this stress. The list below is by no means complete but provides some suggestions for stress management.

1. Get sufficient sleep. If the elderly relative's nocturnal wandering becomes a chronic problem, ask the physician for medication to help induce sleep in the elderly person. Loss of sleep for the caregiver can lead to decreased emotional control and judgment. The quality of care is likely to suffer, and the caregiver may experience greater stress and guilt.

2. Take time off away from the home. The family caregiver should not become trapped in the home attending to the elderly relative. If other relatives or friends can sit with the person or a network of relatives can provide occasional weekend relief, the arrangement should be made on a regular basis. The caretaker needs time off periodically.

3. Join support organizations. Self-help and support groups for those taking care of elderly impaired relatives can be found in almost every community. Organizations such as the Alzheimer's Disease and Related Disorders Association can often provide group facilitators to begin new support networks. These groups offer families emotional support, information on diseases and medications, practical suggestions for behavior management, and ideas for coping with stress.

4. Maintain as many personal interests as possible. The caretaker should keep up with as many friends, hobbies, outside interests, and activities as feasible. It is not a good practice to focus solely on the needs of the elderly relative. The caretaker should attempt to maintain a balance between personal interests and the requirements of caring for the elderly relative.

5. Exercise regularly. Exercise, particularly vigorous exercise, can help alleviate both depression and stress. It provides a healthy outlet for emotional tensions that may build up throughout the day.

6. Keep a diary or some type of daily record to identify situations that are particularly stressful. The clinician may be

helpful in suggesting ways to record information through the day. These situations can then be analyzed with the clinician to determine how they might be modified to relieve the stressful factors.

7. Prepare contingency plans for the care of the elderly relative should the caretaker become incapacitated. The network mentioned earlier might serve the dual purpose of relieving the primary caretaker and acting as a buffer to allow for appropriate nursing home placement if the caretaker can no longer provide adequate care.

Outpatient Assessment

At times the family of the impaired elderly person may consult with the mental health professional in an outpatient setting. They may be aware of the relative's mental problems but may not understand the cause or how to manage the resulting behaviors.

The clinician can use the geriatric assessment form for the initial screening (see Exhibit 3.2 in Chapter 3). This form will provide information regarding the individual's general mental status. If depression is a possible factor in the impairment, the clinician might administer a screening test for depression. The test or scale used, however, should be constructed for a geriatric population, similar to the Geriatric Depression Scale devised by Brink, Yesavage, Lum, Heersema, Adey, and Rose (1982). The clinician should also take a detailed history of the elderly person, paying particular attention to how rapidly symptoms appeared and to any related psychological problems in the past.

The mental health professional should then make sure the elderly person is given a comprehensive physical examination complete with lab work and neurological tests. Permission to release information should be obtained from the family so that results of psychological assessment and history can be shared with medical professionals. Also, the clinician should share information with the family regarding drug side-effects and the management of various problem behaviors including wandering, agitation, combativeness, and inappropriate sexual behavior. (See Appendices C, D, E, and F.)

Nursing Home Placement

In some cases, the clinician may be called upon to help the family decide whether to place the elderly relative in a nursing home.

This decision is frequently painful and may cause family members to feel angry and guilt-ridden. In this section, we discuss various counseling techniques that can be used to help the family make such a decision. It is paramount, however, that family members confront the situation honestly and directly. The problem-solving process advocated by D'Zurilla and Goldfried (1971) is one way to provide a framework for discussing the decision.

This process involves a method of analyzing a problem in a step-by-step fashion to preclude an impulsive course of action. The authors suggest the following steps in the problem-solving process:

1. Problem definition and formulation, which includes a complete and detailed description of the situation, goals, and conflicts that make it a problem.
2. Generating a number of alternative general strategies (i.e., brainstorming).
3. A decision-making phase in which the implementation of various strategies is evaluated in terms of long- and short-term consequences.

The clinician can prepare for such eventualities by becoming familiar with the nursing homes in the area, their admissions policies, costs, programs, staffing, and the like. Family members are likely to be too emotionally involved to make an objective, detached evaluation of the homes. They will look to the mental health professional for guidance.

One of the first considerations is cost. Before a nursing home can be selected, the family must realistically estimate what they can afford and their available sources of funds. Both federal and state programs exist that can provide financial assistance, at least in part. Medicare usually provides funds for clients who require a significant amount of nursing care. Unfortunately, the elderly demented person with no serious medical problems is often denied such assistance because the care required is only custodial. Also, to qualify, recipients must be 65 years of age and eligible for social security.

Medicaid is a second source of financial assistance. The plan is administered through the state and will often cover what Medicare does not. Eligibility is based on the elderly person's needs and assets. The local departments of health, public welfare, or human resources can provide information about the program.

Once appropriate funding is secured, the level of care for the elderly person must be established. Will extensive nursing care, physical therapy, surgery, or other medical procedures be needed for the patient? A physician should evaluate the patient's needs and forward the information to the state department, which then determines the appropriate level of care. The local department of health or welfare will provide information on the correct procedure and the department that has responsibility for determining the level of care.

Once the level of care and funding issues have been settled, the process of selecting the best home can begin. The clinician should draw up a list of nursing homes that offer services matching the elderly person's and the family's needs. Before scheduling a visit to any of these homes, the clinician and family should consult with the local regulatory authority to be sure the facility and administrators are properly licensed. It may also be helpful to check with the local commission on aging or senior citizens council for information regarding selected facilities.

The clinician or family can then make arrangements with the administrators of several nursing homes to visit the sites. When touring a facility, probe for the following information.

1. Is the facility part of any program that monitors standards of care like the Long-Term Care Council of the Joint Commission on Accreditation of Hospitals?
2. Is there any voluntary participation in peer review?
3. What is the rate of staff turnover? A high turnover may indicate a morale problem, which can affect the quality of care given.

    What kinds of activity programs are offered? Are they varied? What are the qualifications of the activity director? This is an important point. Often activity directors will have other duties in the facility and will be selected to plan and conduct resident activities on the basis of criteria other than formal training. As a result, they may not be properly qualified for the job.
5. What are the resident-to-staff ratios of both aides and licensed personnel on all shifts? As the ratio becomes higher, staff may be less able to provide personalized care and to monitor residents. Compare the ratios of several facilities.
6. What are the qualifications and reputations of the consulting physicians? Have they had special training in geriatric medicine and in the use of psychotropic

medications? If possible, talk with families of current residents about their views of the competence of consulting physicians.

7. Is there a working relationship between the nursing home and local mental health center? Nursing home populations in general are woefully underserved in the area of mental health. Nursing homes that have a consulting psychologist or psychiatrist are the exception.

8. Are current residents of the facility and their families satisfied with meal selection and quality? This is a critical concern for residents who will need special diets.

9. Are residents allowed to bring personal items with them such as their own furniture? Elderly persons usually have a favorite chair, rug, bedside table, or other items. Bringing such personal possessions with them can help in the transition from home and create a more intimate atmosphere in a frequently sterile environment.

10. How does the nursing home handle problem behavior? Question the staff about how they typically deal with wandering, combative behavior, noncompliance, and the like.

11. To what degree can the resident and the family participate in choosing a roommate? Nothing can be more distressing to an elderly person than to have an incompatible roommate or one who is so demented that behavior management is a serious problem.

In addition to finding out the above information, the family, when touring a nursing home, should also look for the following.

1. Are most of the residents in their rooms or are they engaged in activities, talking in groups, and the like? The level of involvement will give families some idea of the emphasis placed on activity programming.

2. Is the facility decorated attractively and are personal articles visible in residents' rooms?

3. Is there a strong odor in the facility? If the odor of urine permeates the air it may indicate there are not enough staff to keep residents and the environment clean.

4. Where are the staff located and what are they doing? The amount of interaction between residents and staff may indicate how resident-centered the facility is.

5. Is there a resident library, garden, or other area where activities take place? Look for activities that seek to stimulate residents' mental and physical abilities.

If possible, have the family visit the facility more than once during different shifts to obtain a balanced view of the home's operations. Suggest that family members ask shift personnel how they like their work and to explain the nature of their jobs. The answers should indicate how oriented they are to the residents.

Transition from Home to Nursing Facility

Few tasks are more difficult for many families than moving the elderly relative to a nursing home. Some families attempt to ease the burden by telling their relatives the move is only temporary or by saying the move is just a visit. They then deposit the relative at the home and leave, depending on the nursing staff to handle the relative's subsequent reactions.

These tactics make the transition considerably more difficult and may do irreparable damage to the relationship between the relative and other family members. Avoid these approaches at all cost. It may be unrealistic to expect that the elderly relative will accept the move to a nursing home quietly. However, the family should discuss the move frankly with the relative and undertake the transition in a timely and thoughtful manner. The following suggestions can help ease the transition from private care to nursing home.

1. Take the elderly relative for a visit to the nursing home. If confusion is a problem for the person, visit the facility at a time when there is little activity. Should a visit be impossible, take snapshots of the home to show the relative.
2. Take some of the relative's personal belongings such as a favorite chair, television, bedside table, or family pictures. Attempt to create a "homey" atmosphere without making the room cluttered.
3. Purchase and install a night light if one is not available in the room. The elderly person waking up at night in unfamiliar surroundings may become confused and frightened.
4. Family visits should be frequent immediately following admission. Over time, the number of visits can be reduced as decided on by the family.
5. On the day of admission, the family should visit with the elderly relative for 1 to 2 hours if possible. When leaving, the family should say their goodbyes quickly and depart. If the elderly relative attempts to cling to particular family

members (daughter, son, grandchild), those members should leave as quickly as possible, giving minimal attention to the behavior.

If the family is concerned that the clinging behavior cannot be managed by themselves, nursing staff should be alerted to the time the family will leave and be on hand to help if necessary. Family members may also enlist the help of family friends who are less emotionally involved and may be able to handle the situation. In addition, mental health professionals such as a social worker or psychologist may be consulted during the transition period to obtain their support and help in managing the change.

With the proper attention to both the elderly relative's needs and the family's emotional reactions, the clinician can help ease the transition from private home to nursing facility for all those concerned.

Appendix A

Behavior Therapy Module: Increasing Appropriate Behavior

This module describes several methods used to increase appropriate or adaptive responses in clients over an entire ward or unit. These techniques have been used successfully in a variety of institutional and private care settings. Aides or staff members can learn these techniques in a short time and apply them to many types of client behaviors. The methods discussed in this module are prompting, stimulus enhancement, primary reinforcement, token economies, behavioral contracts, and a behavior level system.

Prompting

Prompting involves the use of verbal or physical cues—or a combination of both—to encourage a particular behavior in a client. One of its principal advantages is that prompting requires the least amount of staff time to administer. Prompting intervenes at the antecedent point rather than at the consequence level. That is, staff can help shape an appropriate response rather than waiting for a behavior to occur, then intervening through some form of positive reinforcement.

Prompts can be used in many situations. For example, staff can guide clients to bring a spoon of food up to their mouths rather than having staff members spoon-feed them. A client can be physically prompted to leave the dorm area and attend an activity, or a staff member can use a gesture to tell a client to get up off the floor. The sequence generally follows three steps: (1) a prompt is given, (2) the behavior occurs, and (3) positive reinforcement is provided immediately.

Prompting not only has the advantage of requiring less staff time but also may help to encourage an appropriate response when an inappropriate one is just as likely to occur. For example, if a staff member sees a client trespassing into the locker or bed area of another client and knows that similar behavior has led to fighting in the past, the staff member can intervene *before* an incident occurs. The client can be given a verbal prompt to leave or, if necessary, guided physically away from the area. Thus, a simple prompt can avoid physical aggression entirely. It is not wise to wait for a fight to break out and then intervene, possibly after someone has been injured.

However, prompts may not be effective for clients who exhibit extreme confusion, short memory span, aphasia, and disorientation caused by severe brain damage from various disorders such as Alzheimer's disease. These clients may not understand what is said to them or why they are being led from one place to another. It's important to remember that their behavior is not an attempt to gain attention, make staff work harder, or get back at anyone. It is the result of organic impairment and altered perception. Staff members can save themselves considerable frustration if they keep this fact in mind and do not take clients' behavior personally.

Stimulus Enhancement

A variety of cues or "prompts" exists on most units or wards that do not require staff involvement. These visual cues also shape a client's behavior in the same way as the staff's verbal and physical prompts. For example, an ash tray usually prompts a client to place cigarette butts and ashes in that receptacle. Chairs and sofas usually prompt clients to sit or lie down, and the toilet usually prompts toileting behavior.

However, if these prompts are not perceived correctly, the usual behavior sequence will not occur or may occur at the wrong time and place. Some clients in geriatric facilities suffer changes in sensory systems, particularly eyesight and hearing, and in their ability to think, remember, and reason. As a result, their behavior may seem bizarre at times to observers. They may wander about the facility as if they were looking for someone or something, urinate on the floor or in their clothes because they cannot find the toilet, or climb into the wrong beds. They are not doing so necessarily to gain attention. Because their brains cannot process information properly, the appropriate cues no longer elicit the appropriate behavior.

Intervention after or during the course of such behaviors does little good in extremely confused clients. However, the environmental stimuli can be enhanced to help clients recognize and respond to them.

Staff can help by directing clients' attention to the appropriate cues already on the unit or ward or to the special prompts that have been added. Pointing out the bathrooms, directing clients to special symbols on their room doors, or placing special cues on their beds such as brightly colored carpet remnants for the visually impaired will help clients respond appropriately. They can learn not only the correct stimulus-response sequence but also increase their independent behavior.

Primary Reinforcement

Up to this point we have discussed intervening before a behavior occurs either by prompting or by enhancing the stimuli of the environment. These interventions are preferred since they can avoid unfortunate consequences and save staff much time.

In many cases, however, staff will be able to intervene only *after* a response has occurred. The intervention is then designed to shape the client's behavior *in the future*. One way to try increasing appropriate behavior is to provide a primary reinforcer after a desirable target behavior occurs.

Primary reinforcers are items that satisfy a primary physical need such as hunger or thirst and that, when delivered, tend to increase the likelihood that a target behavior will be repeated. Primary reinforcers are used for lower functioning clients for these two reasons.

1. Primaries usually can be delivered immediately after an appropriate response occurs. This is important because lower functioning clients do not learn easily to give a correct response and cannot wait long for positive reinforcement. Clients with a short memory span, for example, would not learn appropriate behavior if they had to wait hours for a token store to open. The connection between response and reinforcement must be immediate.
2. Most primaries such as M&M's, applesauce, or a sip of cola can be consumed rapidly, requiring less staff time to administer. Staff members do not have to wait until the item is smoked, traded in, or digested. This characteristic of primaries is particularly useful for shaping behaviors such as speaking appropriately, not yelling, and the like.

Some clients do not require the immediate delivery of a primary system and can learn to respond correctly even when reinforcement is delayed several hours or days. However, it is still wise to give these clients some reinforcer immediately after the target behavior occurs even if the item cannot be consumed until later.

Token Economy

A token economy involves delivering tokens or points to clients after a desired behavior has occurred. These tokens or points can then be cashed in for primary reinforcers or other favorite items. Token economies can be effective with higher functioning clients on a ward for several reasons.

1. Token slips, poker chips, or signature cards are less cumbersome to carry and deliver than primary reinforcers, particularly since different clients often prefer different reinforcers.
2. When clients consume enough of the primary reinforcer, they will stop responding. They have no motivation to obtain more food or drink if they are satiated. With tokens, however, clients never get "filled up" because they can pick out the desired items only when the token store is open. In addition, tokens may be like money in that clients feel they never have enough.
3. The number of tokens that are traded in can be counted more easily than the number of sips of cola or the number of spoons of applesauce. This is helpful in the evaluation of a client's progress under treatment. Counting the number of reinforcers given reflects the number of times the target response occurred.
4. Acquiring and trading tokens resembles the real-world economy in which people are expected to work for 2 weeks or a month before receiving their "pay." They exchange paper money (secondary reinforcers) for food (primary reinforcers), and people often delay the trade-in until they can cash their checks and get to the store. These are important lessons for clients to learn before they are discharged into the community. They need to understand that they will not receive primary reinforcement for each appropriate behavior and that they must delay reinforcement in many instances. Taking part in a token economy

will give them experience in trading items and delaying reinforcement.

5. Tokens are easier than primaries to subtract as a penalty. If a response cost program is used to reduce an inappropriate behavior, it is easier to deduct tokens than to try to take back something the client has half eaten or drunk.

Behavioral Contracts

Contracts can be used to increase appropriate responses and at the same time decrease inappropriate ones. We engage in many written and verbal contracts in daily life, often without thinking about them. They may range from the informal (an invitation to dinner that will be reciprocated in the future) to the formal (a mortgage contract).

These contracts can be defined as agreements between two parties that stipulate the behavior required of each side. For instance, if Party X does something (or refrains from doing something), then Party Y will do something (or refrain from doing something) for Party X. You might make a contract with your children that if they clean their rooms, take out the garbage, and do the dishes, you will give them an allowance, allow television time, and let them stay up later on weekends.

A *behavioral contract* between client and staff is no different. Both parties know exactly what is expected of them, the time period covered, and the payment to be given at the end. (A sample contract form and a completed contract are presented at the end of this appendix.) For example, a client and staff member may draw up a contract to increase the client's self-grooming behavior. The stated time period of the contract might be 4 weeks and the payment at the end free access to token store supplies or canteen items. Another client might instead be promised an industrial therapy or a workshop assignment in payment for decreasing combative behavior.

When making contracts with clients, it may be preferable to provide short- and long-term reinforcers. The staff member contracting with the client to increase self-grooming behavior might provide additional tokens as immediate reinforcement. If the desired behavior is maintained for a week, the client may be allowed to cash in some of the tokens on a limited basis at the token store. At the end of the contract time, the client would be given the long-term payment agreed upon: unlimited access to the token store. Long-term reinforcers encourage clients to maintain the desired behavior over longer periods of time, which will be necessary outside the structured institutional setting. Short- or long-term reinforcers should be given immediately upon clients' fulfillment of the contract conditions.

Clients should be encouraged to help write the contract and decide on reinforcement, length of time, and target behaviors. Their motivation to fulfill contract requirements will be higher if they have had some hand in drawing up the conditions.

To summarize, the following points should be considered in writing behavioral contracts.

1. *The behavior required of clients should be specified to minimize disagreements between clients and staff.* The exact behavior desired (increase in self-feeding, making the bed; decrease in combativeness, inappropriate speech) should be specified in detail in the contract. It is not enough to say "The client will engage in appropriate behavior and not engage in inappropriate behavior." The two parties to the contract must agree on a target behavior.

2. *The time limit should be specified in the contract.* Specific deadlines should be mentioned: "The client will bathe, shave, and dress by 9:00 a.m. each day for 2 weeks in order to earn a weekend pass home." This is preferable to a less specific time: "The client will bathe, shave, and dress by 9:00 a.m. in order to earn a weekend pass home." Without a specific time period, the association between behavior change and reinforcement is less clear. The client does not know when the contract is fulfilled, and there is likely to be considerable debate between the two parties about contract conditions.

3. *Reinforcement should be specified.* Rewards for the target behavior should be listed specifically: "The client will be given a locker key on the fifteenth." "The client will receive a weekend pass home after 1 week of perfect attendance at physical therapy sessions." Again, when rewards are stated and agreed upon by both parties to the contract, arguments about reinforcement can be avoided.

4. *Short- and long-term goals should be included for clients who have difficulty delaying reinforcement.* Some clients cannot delay reinforcement for appropriate behavior for an entire week unless they have a smaller reward each day. In

such cases, the contract should specify both short- and long-term reinforcement. This short-term reinforcement might involve access to token store supplies, extra points within the token economy, a primary reinforcer, or some other immediate reward. Long-term or delayed reinforcement is more similar to conditions outside the institutional setting. The system can be used to help clients become accustomed to a schedule of reinforcement that is likely to exist at home or in the community. Clients are likely to be less frustrated, and the desired behavior should continue at relatively the same rate.

Behavior Level System

The behavior level system is a built-in reinforcement program and goes hand in hand with the behavioral contracting system. Within a behavior level system a client's behavior is consequated by a drop or rise in a numbered level. For example, a client on the highest level with the most privileges may be dropped a level for engaging in fighting.

Clients would be given various consequences depending on whether they moved up or down a level in behavior. It is not the change in levels, per se, that acts as a reinforcer but the privileges associated with the levels. Access to the canteen, an off-ward job, outside time, and the like can be powerful reinforcers, especially for clients in a locked ward. Level changes and the attendant rewards should be contingent on clients demonstrating the desired behavior and should be delivered immediately for maximum effect.

Clients working within a level system should be given the behavior expected at each level and the criteria for advancement. When clients know the entire system, and how they can move up the behavioral "ladder," they can start working to increase their level from the day they are admitted.

CONTRACT

If _____ does the following:
   (the client)

_____
   (behavior required of client)

_____

_____

From _____
   (period beginning)

To _____
   (period ending)

Then _____ will
   (staff contracting)

_____
   (behavior required of staff)

_____

_____

_____

Approved by: _____ Date: _____
          Staff

_____ Date: _____
          Client

SAMPLE CONTRACT

If _Mr. Baxley_ does the following:
   (the client)

Attends 75% of scheduled activities
(behavior required of client)

and does not have any episodes of combativeness,
begging, or verbal abuse.

From _August 16, 1985_
   (period beginning)

To _August 30, 1985_
   (period ending)

Then _Ms. Dunaway, SPI_ will
   (staff contracting)

Raise level from III-C to II-A and
(behavior required of staff)
the client will receive all the
privileges of level II-A.

Approved by: _Carolyn Dunaway_   Date: _8-15-85_
   Staff

           N. Baxley   Date: _8-15-85_
   Client

Appendix B

Behavior Therapy Module: Decreasing Inappropriate Behavior

Inappropriate behaviors exhibited by some clients in geriatric facilities may occur at a frequency and intensity that can become annoying and even dangerous. Such behaviors may prevent clients from being discharged to less restrictive settings or may result in former residents being readmitted from a home or community environment to an institution.

Behavior therapy techniques can be applied successfully to many of these problem behaviors. The same methods can be used with geriatric and younger patients, since many of the problems exhibited by both are similar. There are a few special considerations that must be taken into account, however, for elderly clients.

In many institutions, a significant percentage of the elderly client population will have Alzheimer's disease (or progressive dementia). This disease strikes about 8% of the elderly population and involves tissue damage in the brain. An individual's memory and normal functions gradually deteriorate as the disease progresses. Clients may show such symptoms as confusion; disorientation regarding time, place, and people; severe memory loss; shortened attention span; agitation; hallucinations; wandering; aimless repetitive behavior such as rubbing table tops, picking at imaginary objects, and taking clothes off and on; furniture rearrangement; voiding in inappropriate places; inappropriate sexual behavior; jiggling door knobs; and eating inedible objects.

While many of these behaviors are bothersome, standard behavioral interventions may not be appropriate because of the organic cause of the problem. For example, giving tokens for finding the right bed may not be enough to shape the client's behavior if the person cannot remember what the tokens represent. The bed may also have to be marked with a bright color or some other individualized symbol to help the client locate the right bed.

These clients also may have been reinforced for particular behavioral patterns for a long time. A lengthy reinforcement history makes it difficult to change the behavior quickly. Caregivers may be tempted to give up trying to modify clients' inappropriate behavior, believing the patients are simply too old or too brain damaged to change.

However, the clients' responses need to be modified for the following reasons:

1. The behavior is one reason the client is in the institution. If the individual is ever to return to a less restrictive placement, the caregiver or mental health professional must at least attempt to change the problem response.

2. The client is living in a facility with others and may disrupt the treatment provided to other clients. The problem behavior must be controlled to whatever degree possible so that treatment for other clients is not disturbed.

3. In some states, staff are mandated by state law to provide *active* treatment for clients regardless of any personal feelings about a client's prognosis or chances for discharge. No individual staff member can decide unilaterally which clients are capable or incapable of benefiting from treatment. The only ethical and legal way to make such a decision is by providing active treatment and trying every possible plan to change a client's behavior. The results of treatment can then be studied by the treatment team to determine whether a client's responses have in fact changed. A staff member or team of staff members does not make this decision without considering treatment outcome data.

4. In some cases, the problem behavior may be aggravated by depression. Depression is the number one nonorganic problem exhibited in an elderly population. Poor health, recent retirement, loss of a loved one or close friends, declining memory and functioning, relocation, and other causes can bring on depression. It can be present even in clients diagnosed with progressive dementia. As a result, the client may look and act even more "senile" than the organic damage would warrant.

Staff should be alert for the signs of depression in all clients. These symptoms in the elderly patient include weight loss, poor appetite, changes in sleep patterns, low activity level, motor slowing, and withdrawal. Staff should always keep in mind that the severely depressed client looks very much like a demented client. The difference is that depression can be treated while dementia is a progressive condition that cannot be reversed.

5. Elderly clients have more physical illnesses and consume more drugs than most clients. Both these conditions can affect clients' behavior. Staff members should be particularly careful to look for physical causes when elderly clients suddenly become agitated or depressed, begin talking to themselves, or act in some uncharacteristic or bizarre manner. Paranoia, hyperactivity, depression, hallucinations, agitation, sudden verbal or vocal outbursts, and self-abuse are often behavioral signs of an underlying physical problem. Disorders such as seizures, congestive heart failure, myocardial infarction, tumors, diabetes, decreased potassium, impactions, infections, fever, anemia, thyroid conditions, pain, chronic obstructive pulmonary disease, and strokes almost always have a psychological component. At times, the psychological symptoms may appear *before* the physical ones.

The caregiver, whether staff or mental health professional, should keep track of how suddenly the changes in behavior occur. Behavior problems caused by physical disorders can be confused easily with those attributed to dementia. If the client is treated for a psychotic condition when the real cause is physical, the treatment will be ineffective, and the true condition will not be uncovered and treated. Staff should always explore the possibility that a physical cause may underlie sudden and severe behavioral changes in clients.

The behavioral techniques described in this section can be used with any high-frequency or high-intensity behavior such as yelling; demanding; making multiple somatic complaints without any physical cause; continually requesting medication, food, or other items; fighting; cursing or making verbal threats; threatening others physically; being sexually aggressive; kicking; biting; engaging in self-abuse; using smoking materials improperly; spitting; and inappropriate voiding. The techniques discussed are extinction, time out, correction, response cost, restriction, and aversive programs.

Extinction

Extinction is a procedure whereby an inappropriate behavior is followed by *no reinforcement* from the observer. The particular response gradually disappears or is extinguished by the lack of reinforcement. For example, a client may repeatedly request cigarettes or call a staff member a vulgar name. Reinforcement would include *any* response to the behavior such as glaring at the client, arguing back, giving in to the request, or trying to teach a more appropriate response. These are all forms of positive reinforcement and, when applied contingently after the inappropriate behavior, they increase the likelihood that the behavior will be repeated later.

Extinction (ignoring a behavior) must be applied carefully and consistently by everyone who comes in contact with the client at the time the behavior occurs. (In fact, it is more difficult in the long run to decrease an inappropriate behavior if it has been ignored by most people and reinforced by only a few. The client is accustomed to being ignored by the others.) Also, staff should realize that for a short time after extinction is first used, the inappropriate behavior may actually get worse before it disappears. Understanding this fact can keep staff members from becoming discouraged at the outset.

The extinction procedure may simply involve staff members turning their backs on the client or moving away from the person without acknowledging that the behavior has been noticed. Staff must decide which behaviors will be targeted for extinction and ensure that everyone involved applies the technique consistently.

Time Out

Time out is a form of extinction that involves placing clients who exhibit inappropriate behavior in an area where they do not receive any form of reinforcement (attention) for their actions. Some clients may be disruptive in a group setting and derive attention from several people. As a result, moving away from the client will not be enough, since the reinforcement comes from more than one person. Or their behavior may provoke other clients to act out their own inappropriate responses such as shouting, cursing, threatening, and the like.

In such cases, the problem client must be removed from the group setting. Staff members can use two forms of time out which differ in their degree of isolation and restriction. The two forms are dorm or corner time out and room time out.

Dorm or Corner Time Out

In cases of verbal threats and abusiveness or other disruptive verbal behavior directed toward the staff or other clients, or when extinction has failed, the client should be prompted to stand or sit in an isolated corner or go into a bay area (dorm time out). Minimal prompting is desirable. If physical guidance is necessary, keep it to a minimum to avoid inadvertently reinforcing the target behavior through touch. Clients should be told the reason for time out, the length of time they will be in isolation, and the criteria for release.

> "Mr. (Mrs., Ms.) _____ , you have been verbally abusive. You are to stay in this corner (dorm) until you have been calm and quiet for 5 minutes."

Anything more than this brief explanation (e.g., arguing with the client, asking for reasons, trying to change the behavior) may be reinforcing the inappropriate behavior.

The client is to stay in corner or dorm time out for as long as it takes to be quiet for 5 continuous minutes. Usually this involves 5 minutes of time, but an upper limit of several hours may be necessary. An observer should note any inappropriate response on a problem behavior sheet, which would also include the time of the incident, the name of the client, the circumstances, the problem behavior, and intervention used.

Usually corner or dorm time out is sufficient. However, staff members should be prepared to take the next step—room time out—if the client is physically aggressive against staff or other clients while attempting to leave the corner or dorm time out or begins to throw or damage furniture in the area. Also, room time out should be used immediately for any problem behavior that involves physical aggression.

Room Time Out

At least one room should be designated as a time-out area on each floor in a facility. The room should be empty so that no reinforcement is available to clients. If a client is sexually aggressive or uses biting, hitting, kicking, slapping, punching, or other types of fighting, the individual should be prompted to enter the time-out room. The client also may be placed in room time out for the following behaviors:

1. Being physically aggressive when attempting to leave corner or dorm time out before the time is up. Such behavior should be recorded as a separate incident on the problem behavior sheet.
2. Being physically resistant during treatment, when given medication or having vital signs taken, or during bathing or dressing. Resistance in this case is defined as aggression. Running away or simply stepping back while being bathed, for example, would not be classified as physical resistance. However, striking a staff member or throwing medication across the room would constitute aggressive physical resistance.
3. Being verbally abusive and threatening to others, particularly when such behavior has been documented as leading to physical aggression. The decision to place a client in room time out is made by the treatment team after reviewing the client's record; it is not made by individual staff members. Staff should use minimal prompts to get the client to enter the time-out room. Physical guidance, if necessary, should also be minimal, just enough to get the client into the room.

When implementing room time out, staff should observe the following procedures:

1. Tell the client the reason time out is being applied. The explanation should be simple and brief. Give the criteria for release and the length of time to be spent in isolation.
2. Check the client for potentially dangerous items such as sharp or hard objects, matches, glass, and the like and remove these items.
3. Check the client for potentially reinforcing objects such as cigarettes, food, reading materials, and the like and remove these items. Time out is not meant to be punishing or reinforcing in any way. Its value lies in the fact that it offers no reinforcement of any kind.
4. Document the intervention on a problem behavior sheet and in the client's record.

5. Check on the client from time to time, particularly at the end of the time period, to make sure the person is safe and is meeting the criteria for release.
6. When the criteria have been met, inform the client that time out is over.

Furniture or items such as a mattress and blanket do not have to be given to the client in time out. In fact, such items may be reinforcing for many residents and should be removed prior to placing a client in the room.

Staff should document when the client met the criteria for leaving time out. If the client leaves the time-out room before the mandatory period or pushes open the door to look out, staff can add on to the client's time or move the client to a more restrictive isolation area.

However, when you lock the time-out room door or move the client to a special seclusion room with a mattress and blanket, the procedure is no longer a behavior therapy program. The intervention has become a medical one, and the institutional rules for seclusion must be followed to satisfy ethical and legal requirements. No one should be placed in seclusion without first being in room time out, unless the more extreme procedure is authorized by a physician. If room time out is not used first, the reason must be carefully documented.

To summarize, extinction is used first to eliminate a client's repeated verbal requests or abusiveness. If the verbal behavior is threatening or extreme, or if extinction is ineffective, dorm or corner time out can be applied. Should the client become physically aggressive in trying to leave time out, damage furniture in the area, or become aggressive prior to time out, room time out is the appropriate intervention. The door is not locked. Only if the client attempts to leave time out prematurely should the door be locked or the patient moved to an area of greater seclusion. Staff should use minimal prompts when applying time-out procedures.

The use of extinction, corner or dorm time out, and room time out do not require a physician's order.

Response Cost

When response cost is used to reduce or eliminate a behavior, the client is told that the targeted behavior will cost the individual some reinforcement. For example, shouting abusively at others may result in some type of "fine." The client must have the reinforcers at hand so that when the inappropriate behavior occurs, part of these reinforcers can be taken away.

A response cost system works particularly well within a token economy. It is relatively easy to remove tokens from a client following an inappropriate response. It is more difficult to remove a primary reinforcer such as food or liquid or a secondary reinforcer like cigarettes. The client is likely to become quite agitated and may use these items or their containers as weapons.

Response cost is used primarily for behaviors that do not involve physical aggression. These behaviors include begging for items, hoarding, possessing contraband, and noncompliance. For example, if a client is discovered to have several cigarettes that belong to another client or staff member, the contraband cigarettes are taken *and* the number of points that would buy the equivalent number of cigarettes are deducted from his total.

This approach is an effective way to reduce stealing and hoarding, behaviors that can undermine any token economy or incentive system. If clients can get reinforcers on their own, they will not be motivated to participate in designated therapies or behavioral treatment programs. With response cost, however, the client loses not only the contraband but also the ability to buy more of the items.

Correction

Correction means prompting a client to restore the environment to its original state before the individual's behavior damaged or rearranged it. The procedure can be carried out on the spot, even when it is not officially part of a client's treatment program.

Correction works well for behaviors such as spitting, inappropriate voiding, and other responses that create some negative change in the environment. These behaviors usually mean that someone must clean the area, and the client should be responsible for restoring the damaged or changed area. The energy clients expend carrying out the task tends to reduce the likelihood that a similar behavior will recur. For example, if a client repeatedly spits on the floor or walls next to the bed, the person should be prompted to clean the area with a towel or mop and to change the linens or bed clothes as needed.

Several important points should be considered in a correction program.

1. Prompt the client to clean only the area damaged. Any

requirement to clean an area beyond that is called *over-correction*. In the authors' facility, overcorrection is considered an aversive program and must be approved by an oversight committee, a treatment team, and the administration of the facility. In addition, the client, if competent and voluntary, must agree to undergo the overcorrection procedure. If the client is incompetent, the person's guardian must consent to the treatment. The program must be monitored and regular reports made to the appropriate authorities.

2. When prompting the client to clean an area, do not argue or engage in conversation. Remember that talking is a positive reinforcer. Simply tell the client to clean the area and see that it is done as quickly and thoroughly as possible.

3. If necessary, physically guide the client's cleaning movements with your hands without doing the client's work. The effort clients must expend is what makes correction effective.

4. Enter the behavior and intervention on the appropriate sheet and in the client's record.

5. If the client physically resists cleaning the mess or uses physical aggression in any way, institute room time out. Note the incident on the problem behavior sheet and in the client's record. If the mess can be left until the client leaves time out, prompt the client to clean or restore the area after time out is over. If the area must be cleaned for client safety, do so and document why correction was not used.

6. Correction can and should be used even with extremely confused geriatric patients who void in the wrong places, unless a documented alternative is provided as a treatment team strategy. The treatment selection should be a team decision, not an individual one. It may be necessary to combine positive practice with the correction procedure for these confused clients. Positive practice after correction entails having clients clean the area and themselves, then practice the correct steps for voiding in the appropriate place.

For example, if a client voids next to the bed, have the person clean the area, with guidance from you if necessary, and change into dry clothes. Next, institute the positive practice phase by leading the client to the rest room, pointing out the toilet, having the person remove the

clothes necessary to void, putting the clothes back on, and
then returning to the bed area. During the practice session, give frequent verbal prompts (e.g., "Here is the toilet
and the toilet paper." "You go past this first door before
coming to the rest room").

Restriction

Restriction, preventing access to a favorite activity or item, is a
fairly straightforward technique. Restrictions are usually applied
to avoid providing positive reinforcement after an inappropriate
behavior. For example, if a client strikes at someone and is given
time out, the person should not then be allowed to go on a field trip
or special outing 10 minutes or an hour later. Even though clients
may receive the appropriate intervention immediately, if they are
then given a major reinforcer soon after, they will have less motivation to give up their problem response and substitute a more
appropriate one.

When used properly, restriction can be a powerful modification tool. If overused, however, it can cause a client to give up and
withdraw completely. Restricting access to tokens, for example,
might mean the client cannot go to the token store for days or even
weeks. This heavy restriction can cause many clients to stop participating in the program and other activities and withdraw from
social contact.

Restrictions are used for behaviors such as fighting, shov-
ing, breaking into line, smoking in inappropriate areas, and the
like. The inappropriate behavior and restriction applied should be
documented by staff on a problem behavior sheet. Restriction can
be used even if it is not part of the client's treatment strategy, provided the team in charge of the client's care is notified of the addition. The team should then review the restriction and decide
whether it should be incorporated into the treatment strategy.

Aversive Programs

Aversive programs are more restrictive interventions that can be
used in special cases to reduce dangerous behavior. These methods include overcorrection (prompting clients to clean not only the
area affected but also a larger area), negative practice (prompting
clients to engage in the inappropriate behavior repeatedly until
they are tired), contingent restraint (placing clients in mechanical or personal restraint as a consequence of inappropriate behav-

ior), and punishment (applying an aversive stimulus to clients such as shock, loud noise, or distasteful substance consequent to an inappropriate behavior).

If such a procedure is deemed necessary by the treatment team within the authors' facility for a particular client and a particular behavior (e.g., self-abuse), several criteria must be met before the intervention can be used. Staff must follow these steps.

1. The treatment team must approve the intervention. This decision should be based upon the seriousness of the behavior and the fact that other, less restrictive alternatives have been shown to be ineffective.
2. If competent, the client must consent to the program. In the case of incompetent clients, a guardian or other legally responsible person must give consent. If no guardian is available, an outside consultant, usually a psychologist, must approve the program.
3. The treatment program must then be approved by an oversight committee and the administrative head of the facility.
4. When all these steps are completed, the program must be carefully monitored by those applying the intervention, all personnel involved must be thoroughly trained, and regular reports of the client's progress sent to the appropriate committees and administrative staff.

Final Remarks

Staff members should keep in mind the following points when involved in behavior therapy treatments.

Whenever a problem behavior is targeted for reduction or extinction, *appropriate or neutral behaviors must be increased or developed at the same time.* It is unethical to reduce a behavior without attempting to replace it with a more appropriate response. The reason for this rule is simple. If an intervention successfully eliminates a certain behavior, the client is left with a gap in time and may easily pick up an even less desirable response to fill the gap. For example, if dorm or corner time out is used to reduce a client's begging for food but no positive reinforcement is given for appropriate verbal responses, the treatment may eliminate the client's talking altogether. Or the client may resort to physical threats to gain the reinforcers that begging brought.

Make sure the consequences fit the inappropriate behavior. Do not overreact to a client's problem responses, especially if you are the target. If the client curses you or calls you names, use extinction first to manage the behavior, not corner time out or restriction of an activity.

No matter which intervention is used to reduce an inappropriate behavior, intervene quickly, consistently, and with minimal touching or conversation. If you cannot act immediately because of various circumstances, it is generally better not to intervene and *document why you could not apply the intervention* than to intervene some 30 minutes or more later. Many clients will not associate a delayed intervention with their inappropriate behavior. To be effective, treatment must establish a clear connection between cause (problem behavior) and effect (intervention).

Appendix C

Drug Education Program for Discharged Clients

The drug education program is designed to help discharged clients maintain their medication schedule and dosage. The medication prescribed by physicians in the facility will help you or your family member function better at home and in the community, provided the same routine is followed. How long such treatment will continue depends on the nature of the problem, the severity of the illness, your physician, and other factors unique to each individual.

We offer the following information not to alarm former clients and their families but to provide guidelines for continuing their medication safely and to list some of the side-effects that may occur. Many drugs affect the elderly population differently than they do younger patients. The physical changes that accompany aging (e.g., loss of functional tissue, decrease in output of the heart, decrease in liver efficiency) can alter the actions of most drugs in the body.

The effects of a drug on behavior and feelings depend on four processes: *absorption* (how the drug is taken into the body), *distribution* (where the drug goes in the body and how long it takes to get there), *metabolism* (where and how fast the drug is broken down into usable chemicals and nonusable waste), and *excretion* (how fast the drug is eliminated from the body). All four processes are affected by the physical changes involved in aging and can alter drug responses.

As a result, we begin this guide with two warnings:

1. *Do not take or allow the client to take more or less of the drug than has been prescribed nor mix the drug with*

someone else's medication. Even if two medicines are prescribed for the same problem, they will not act the same way in each individual. Make sure the medication taken is the one prescribed and is the correct dosage. If the drug seems to have lost its effectiveness or is exerting too much effect, notify a physician.

2. *Follow the prescribed schedule carefully.* If the prescription calls for the drug to be given "as needed" and not on a routine basis, follow the directions. Do not give the medication unless the behavior requires it.

The following section is a simple guide for effective medication consumption. The first part is a list of Do's and Don'ts in taking medication. The second part is a list of commonly prescribed drugs and some of their adverse side-effects. These side-effects are usually rare. However, they can be bothersome enough to warrant a change in medication, or they may indicate that a more serious condition exists. These drug responses can occur in anyone. *They are not allergic reactions.*

We hope that you or your family member will not experience any problems with the medication or with any other aspect of readjustment once outside the hospital. We realize that making the transition is a big step and may be difficult for all concerned. This guide should help eliminate two potential complications of returning to community life: improper consumption of medication and the negative side-effects of the drugs themselves.

GUIDELINES FOR MEDICATION CONSUMPTION

1. Tell your doctor in the community about all of the medications you are taking and about any allergies or side-effects that you may have experienced with any drug.
2. Make sure you thoroughly understand all instructions such as when to take the drug, how many or how much to take, what (if anything) should be taken with the drug, when you should stop the medication, and whom to notify if problems arise.
3. Keep a record of the drugs you are taking. A calendar or some other type of time sheet may be useful in keeping track of when you are to take your medication. If you think you have forgotten to take a particular drug at the proper time, do not try to double up on medication without first consulting your doctor.
4. Call your doctor if you notice any new side-effects.
5. Keep drugs in their original airtight containers and store them in the appropriate place to maintain their potency.
6. When you visit your doctor or mental health facility, bring your drugs or at least a list of all drugs you are taking and the amounts of each you have left in the containers. Your list should include nonprescription medicines such as cough syrup, aspirin, nasal sprays, laxatives, and many other over-the-counter drugs. These medicines can affect the way your prescribed drugs work in your body.
7. Write down instructions concerning how to take each drug. Do not rely on memory. Refer to these instructions any time you are in doubt about dosage and medication schedule.
8. Do not substitute one drug for another unless told to do so by your pharmacist or doctor. Drugs designed to have similar effects can act quite differently in *your* body.
9. Do not mix medications with alcohol unless your doctor has said it is all right to do so.
10. Keep different medications on different shelves in your medicine cabinet. If you haven't enough room, at least keep them far enough apart on each shelf that you cannot accidentally pick up the wrong medication.
11. Do not stop taking your medication even when you feel better unless you have obtained your doctor's permission.

COMMONLY PRESCRIBED DRUGS AND POTENTIAL SIDE-EFFECTS

Class	Medication Generic	Brand	Side-effects	Comments
Antiarthritic	Indomethacin Sulindac	Indocin Clinoril	Depression, con- fusion, paranoia, hallucinations	Especially in the elderly
Anticonvulsant	Phenobarbital Phenytoin Primidone	 Dilantin Mysoline	Hallucinations, delirium, confusion, lethargy, depression	Usually with high doses
Antidepressant	Amitriptyline Desimpramine Doxepin Imipramine Nortriptyline Protriptyline	Elavil Norpramin Adapin, Sinequan Tofranil Aventyl Vivactil	Anticholinergic psychosis, agitation, sedation, dry mouth, urinary retention, constipation	
Antihypertensive & Diuretic	Chlorthalidone Clonidine Furosemide Hydralazine Hydrochlorothiazide Methyldopa Reserpine Spironolactone	Hygroton Catapres Lasix Apresoline Hydrodiuril Aldomet In Ser-Ap-Es In Aldactazide	Lethargy, depression, sexual disturbances, headache	
Antiparkinson	Amantadine Benztropine Carbidopa & Levodopa	Symmetrel Cogentin Sinemet	Visual hallucinations, nightmares, atropine psychosis	See atropine

Category	Generic	Brand	Symptoms	Conditions
Atropine & Anticholinergic	Includes the antidepressants, some antiparkinsons, and some major tranquilizers		Confusion, memory loss, delirium, acute psychosis, hallucinations, anxiety	
Major tranquilizers	Chlorpromazine	Thorazine	Drowsiness, sedation, restlessness, tremor, muscle tics, rigidity, mouth movements, tongue darting, obesity	Especially in the elderly
	Fluphenazine	Prolixin		
	Haloperidol	Haldol		
	Mesoridazine	Serentil		
	Thioridazine	Mellaril		
	Thiothixene	Navane		
	Trifluoperazine	Stelazine		
Minor tranquilizers	Clorazepate	Tranxene	Sedation, depression, confusion, anorexia, psychotic behavior on abrupt withdrawal, excitement	May occur at usual doses
	Chlordiazepoxide	Librium		
	Diazepam	Valium		
	Hydroxyzine	Atarax, Vistaril		
	Oxazepam	Serax		
Others	Corticosteroids (prednisone, cortisone, etc.)		Psychotic behavior, confusion, paranoia, hallucinations	Excessive doses
	Ephedrine		Hallucinations	
	Lidocaine	Xylocaine	Disorientation	
	Methylphenidate	Ritalin	Hallucinations	
	Pentazocine	Talwin	Nightmares, hallucinations, panic, depression, paranoia	

COMMONLY PRESCRIBED DRUGS *(continued)*

| Class | Medication | | Side-effects | Comments |
	Generic	Brand		
Others	Phenylephrine	Neo-Synephrine	Depression, hallucinations, paranoia	Overuse
	Procainamide	Pronestyl	Paranoia, hallucinations	Not common
	Proposyphene	Darvon	Hallucinations, confusion	Higher doses

We will circle the drug(s) which you will be taking at discharge. Please keep this chart in a convenient place even after these discharge medications are finished.

Name _____

Medication _____ Amount _____ Times

Medication _____ Amount _____ Times

Medication _____ Amount _____ Times

Appendix D
Discharge Program: Wandering

The patient (client) whom we are discharging into your care has shown a tendency to wander through the hallways while residing at our facility. We realize that such behavior may have serious consequences or cause problems primarily because you cannot lock your exit doors. The procedures discussed in this program may help reduce or confine such behavior.

Wandering can be defined as ambulation or wheel-chair-assisted movement that appears to be independent of environmental stimuli or constraints (EXIT signs, room numbers, warning signs, and the like). Often wanderers cannot tell you where they are going, or they may respond inappropriately (e.g., going home, going hunting, looking for mother or other people). They will also show other signs of confusion or disorientation and may have physical disorders such as organic brain syndrome (OBS), organic mental disorder (OMD), or senile dementia.

Research has shown that wanderers cannot be lumped into one category and that they often respond to attempts to modify their wandering. Below, we describe four types of wanderers you are likely to encounter in any elderly population. We have circled the number that best describes the client's behavior.

Categories of Wanderers

1. Some elderly individuals who show general confusion, disorientation, and lack of personal skills appear to ambulate constantly as a form of stimulation. They may also exhibit other kinds of self-stimulation such as door-knob rattling, clapping, repetitious vocalizations, rocking,

rubbing themselves or table tops, and patting walls, furniture, or pictures on the wall. They may engage in these behaviors to gain a certain level of stimulation that, with their brain dysfunction and other changes, the outside world may no longer provide. Similar behavior has been observed in severely retarded children and adults, autistic children, infants reared in unstimulating environments, and animals raised in isolation.

2. Some wanderers appear to be seeking a way out of the facility. These clients are often, though not always, new residents and want to leave. Or they may be extremely confused and believe that the ward or facility is their previous home, work place, or hospital. This type of wanderer may prove the most difficult to manage, particularly for the first few months of residence. If they escape observation for even a short time, they may slip away and even manage to leave the facility. Once outside they can become very difficult to find.

3. Some wanderers are not really wanderers in the true sense but are simply continuous ambulators or pacers. Their ambulation is often the result of long-term use of certain major tranquilizers. These clients typically enter an unlocked or opened door accidentally during their pacing, although the results can be the same as an intentional act if they are unobserved and become lost or leave the residence.

4. The final class of wanderers may overlap slightly with the previous three categories. These wanderers engage in the behavior only with others. They have no intention of leaving the residence or entering prohibited areas, but they will do so if the person they are with goes through the door. Their level of confusion varies, which would affect your choice of behavioral techniques used to modify their responses.

Strategies for Managing Wandering

In this section we present some management techniques that have reduced wandering in the four classes of wanderers defined above. We have circled the one(s) we think would help the client. Please note that more than one approach may be needed, at least temporarily, to manage wandering.

1. *Sensory extinction.* Used with Category 1 wanderers. This technique seeks to remove the source of self-stimulation

that helps maintain the wandering behavior. For example, if the client is rattling door knobs or spinning the knobs more than three or four times or pushing on the door, you might simply tighten the knobs and make sure the door fits better in its frame. This would eliminate the stimulation received when the knob is turned or the door is pressed.

2. *Providing other outlets.* Used with Category 1 and possibly Category 3 wanderers. If self-stimulation appears to be the reason for wandering (Category 1), you might provide a variety of items that can be shaken, rubbed, squeezed, spun, twirled, listened to, smelled, pinched, patted, or otherwise manipulated (although not eaten). These items would provide safer outlets for self-stimulation than wandering and should always be used when you employ Strategy 1.

   With Category 3 wanderers, who often ambulate because they cannot help it, you may offer scheduled times to ambulate when they can be observed more closely. Try not to impede their movements while they are sitting or sleeping.

3. *Instructions.* Used with Category 3 and Category 4 wanderers, but can be applied or at least attempted with all categories. Simply instruct wanderers to ambulate only in designated areas no matter what other ambulators are doing. Stress that particular doors are not to be opened or, if already open, are not to be entered.

4. *Response prevention and extinction.* Used with Category 2 and in conjunction with Strategies 5 and 6 below. Stop the client from entering unauthorized areas, at least for a certain period of time. Given enough time, most clients will no longer attempt to enter these areas or try to leave the residence since they have never been allowed to complete the behavior and receive any positive consequences or reinforcement. If possible, gradually reduce your efforts to prevent certain wandering responses. Be gentle and use the least amount of restraint possible.

   Note: Some Category 2 wanderers, particularly those looking for a nonexistent person or room, may be helped if they are allowed to go into the unauthorized area under your supervision. If they consistently fail to find what they are looking for, they may begin to ignore the area.

5. *Temporary close observation.* Used with all categories. Allow reasonably free ambulation if possible until you feel comfortable with the type of ambulation the client is showing and until the client is adjusted to the new surroundings. Observe the client for the following: presence or absence of other self-stimulatory behavior, the presence or absence of other signs of motor restlessness, verbalizations while wandering, and selection of others with whom the client ambulates. The information gathered can help you decide how to intervene. For example, you may have a Category 4 wanderer who seems to attach only to certain residents that show more dangerous ambulation patterns. As treatment, you can pair two Category 4 wanderers or allow them to ambulate only when the other types of wanderers are not present.

6. *Permanent close observation.* Used primarily with Category 2 and Category 3 wanderers. With Category 2 wanderers, extinction may not always work, forcing you to rely on close supervision during ambulation. With Category 3 wanderers who are particularly confused and restless, instruction alone may not work. They will require constant monitoring during ambulation.

7. *Medication change.* Used under physician's direction with Category 3 wanderers. Usually this type of wanderer has already been tried on less problematic tranquilizers or antiparkinson medications to reduce the drug side-effects (akathisia). However, your physician(s) may have had success with other drugs or dosages and wish to try them.

8. *Temporary guidance with cue.* This is a relatively new technique to be used with all categories but those clients who are determined to leave the residence. Wanderers, no matter how confused they may appear, still respond to simple, brightly colored cues. Symbols in bright colors can be placed on doors to unauthorized areas or hung from the ceiling before the EXIT door or painted on the floor in front of the EXIT door.

   The client is then ambulated with minimal assistance up and down the ward to the color cue. If the client crosses the cue, the assistant should gently say "No" and turn the client back. Direct the client's attention to the color cue each time you pass it. If the client turns before the

color cue and EXIT door, offer a positive reinforcer immediately (applesauce, sip of soda, bite of cookie).

You will have to continue this guided ambulation,
pointing out the cue and saying "No" or giving the reinforcement, twice a day for 2 weeks or so. Use Strategy 5
(temporary close observation) in conjunction with this
technique.

Note: Clients discharged from our facility may have
been trained to respond to certain color cues. We will provide a description of these cues or the cues themselves for
you to attach to the designated areas for these clients.

9. *Sedation or restraint.* Used with all wanderers, particularly Category 2. These two techniques are effective in
reducing wandering behavior for all four categories of wanderers. Their disadvantage is that they also tend to reduce
other, more desirable behaviors. At the physician's discre-
tion, however, a temporary reduction in agitation may help
during the adjustment period, especially with Category 2
wanderers.

We hope that this guide will help in the treatment plan for the
client. It should be used as a guide only and not considered as *the*
treatment recommendations for this client. Your attending phy-
sician(s) should order any such programming. If you have any
questions regarding these treatments or the client, please call us.

Appendix E
Discharge Program: Agitation and Combativeness

The patient (client) whom we are discharging into your care has in the past shown combative and agitated behavior. We do not discharge patients who are actively combative or agitated or who have had episodes of these behaviors immediately prior to discharge. However, this patient has been treated for such episodes in the past. In the unlikely event the patient engages in these behaviors again, we have compiled a list of treatment techniques that can be used to reduce such responses. The techniques can also be applied to any patient who shows even a moderate amount of agitation or combativeness.

In the first section we will describe some of the common causes of these episodes. You will then be able to look for these causes when any of your new or current residents become agitated or aggressive. We have circled the number(s) of those factors that have led to such episodes in this client in the past.

Causes of Agitation/Combativeness

1. *Acute organic disturbances.* Physical problems are some of the most common causes of agitation even in clients with no prior history of such behavior. The presence of a variety of physical problems in the elderly may result in agitation, striking out, confusion, and disorientation. These disorders include hyperthyroidism, hyperglycemia, hypercalcemia, viral or bacterial infections, myocardial infarction, congestive heart failure, arrhythmias, vascular insufficiency, trauma, fecal impaction, fractures,

recent surgery or anesthesia, azotemia, cerebral neo-
plasms, Cushing's syndrome, hepatic failure, and unto-
ward side-effects or allergic reactions to medication.

If the onset of symptoms is particularly sudden and if
other physical signs are present (e.g., tachycardia, sweating, confusion), you should suspect one of these causes. In
some instances, however, the agitation will precede the
manifestation of physical symptoms and may actually
serve to alert you to a physical problem in its early stages.

2. *Agitation which accompanies a chronic physical condition.* Two main causes of agitation in this category are agitation secondary to physically induced frustration and
   agitation secondary to hallucinations.

   a. Frustration. Though frustration may lead to agitation
      in anyone, it is usually less intense and dangerous than
      agitation associated with the following disorders fre-
      quently found in the elderly:

      • Cerebrovascular accident or other mobility-limiting
        conditions. Hemiplegia and aphasia may lead to frus-
        tration that can result in the client striking out or
        engaging in verbal abusiveness. It is important to
        realize that the abuse is not aimed at anyone person-
        ally but at whomever happens to be nearby. After the
        client adjusts to the physical limitations, this type of
        agitation and combativeness usually disappears or
        becomes less intense.

      • Alzheimer's disease and related disorders. In the
        early to middle stages of a progressive dementia, the
        individual realizes that memory and functioning are
        diminishing. It can be quite frustrating to find that
        one can no longer remember names and dates, dress
        oneself, balance a checkbook, write legibly, find the
        right word, or locate familiar items. The person may
        even begin to blame family members or staff or accuse
        them of stealing the items. During these phases, agi-
        tation and combativeness are quite common. This
        type of frustration-agitation may resurface periodi-
        cally even in the later stages of the disorder.

   b. Hallucinations associated with Alzheimer's disease
      and related disorders. During the later stages of a pro-
      gressive dementia, many clients become easily upset
      often without any identifiable external cause. While

these episodes may be due to an acute physical problem, as described in Category 1, they may also occur in the absence of such causes. The client appears to be reacting to a visual or auditory hallucination which causes panic and striking out. The client may not readily tell you the source of panic but probing might uncover the presence of the hallucination. Sudden changes in surroundings or routine or rapid movements around the client may provoke the panic/agitation.

3. *Attention-seeking*. Sometimes it is not a precipitating stimulus that causes agitation or combativeness but the consequences that have followed the behavior. Some patients have learned that they can gain a great deal of attention by striking out and becoming abusive. Other methods of attracting attention may have not worked, leaving the patient with only an inappropriate manner of attention-seeking.

Strategies to Manage Agitation and Combativeness

The following techniques have been used successfully to reduce agitation and combativeness. We have circled the number(s) of the methods used to treat the client in the past.

1. *Medical approach*. If the cause for the agitation or combativeness appears to fall into Category 1, the underlying physical condition must be treated. If treatment is successful, the agitation should subside. After recovery, explain to the client the relationship between the physical problem and agitation or combativeness.

2. *Minimize stimulation*. Agitation that falls within Category 1 or 2 may be reduced somewhat by minimizing excessive stimulation. Calming the client, moving slowly, reducing outside noise, and keeping changes to a minimum can decrease the intensity of the episode.

3. *Medication*. Under the attending physician's guidance, the client may be given minor tranquilizers as needed to reduce the frequency and intensity of agitation or combativeness, particularly the type that falls under Category 2b.

4. *Temporary guidance and light restraint*. This technique may be useful with Categories 1 and 2. Lightly restrain the client's arm or leg or other body part being used to strike

out and gently ask the client to stop. Gradually reduce your contact until the episode subsides.

5. *Extinction.* This method is the best approach for Category 3 agitation. You will need the cooperation of the entire staff to apply this technique successfully. If the agitation/combativeness is seen as an attempt to gain attention, the client's behavior should be ignored when the next episode occurs. No one should talk to or reason with, restrain, or bribe the client. Use your best judgment in allowing the behavior to run its course. This approach should be applied only if the client and others are not in danger and only when the behavior is moderate. The reason for such caution is that ignoring the behavior may actually lead to a temporary *increase* in the intensity and frequency of response. Staff must be willing to contend with this short-term increase.

At the same time extinction is applied, you must also provide positive reinforcement (attention) for nonaggressive behavior to increase more appropriate responses. Otherwise, the client may simply replace one inappropriate behavior with another to gain attention.

We hope this program will help in managing the client. While we do not anticipate any agitation or combative episodes, changing from one residence to another may provoke such behavior temporarily. The treatment methods we have circled should enable you to manage the client's behavior. If you have any questions regarding these techniques or the client, please call us.

Appendix F

Discharge Program: Inappropriate Sexual Behavior

The patient (client) whom we are discharging into your care has in the past been treated for exhibiting inappropriate sexual behavior. We do not discharge clients who show this type of behavior prior to leaving, but such problems may arise again when a client changes to a new residence. In addition, increasing confusion caused by acute or progressive brain dysfunction may cause a client to engage in this behavior for the first time after discharge.

In the unlikely event that the client may show these responses, we have summarized some of the causes and treatment strategies for such behavior. We hope to prevent the need to readmit the client to our facility by providing you with programs that have been used successfully to manage inappropriate sexual responses. We have circled the cause(s) below that pertain to the client's history.

Causes of Inappropriate Sexual Behavior

1. *Medication induced.*
    a. Dystonia. Major tranquilizers may cause contraction-release cycles in some muscle groups beyond the voluntary control of the patient. Though this side-effect occurs rarely, when it involves muscles in the upper torso or pelvic regions, observers may "see" inappropriate sexual behavior. Pelvis thrusting that accidentally contacts others may be construed as attempts at sexual contact. When upper muscles are involved, the arms may swing and make accidental contact with

177

another person in an area considered private. Patients with cerebral palsy and Huntington's chorea have similar, involuntary muscle movements.

   b. Confusion. Some medications or combinations of medications may increase the level of confusion in debilitated elderly to the extent that the patient begins to climb into others' beds, expose himself, and the like. If this new behavior coincides with the start or increase of a minor tranquilizer, steroid, or anti-hypertensive drug, suspect the medication.

2. *Cerebrovascular accident-induced disinhibition.* Some post-CVA patients (usually male) will show inappropriate sexual behavior for the first time. This form of behavior differs from that involving poor muscular control and concerns the loss of inhibiting brain functions caused by the stroke. Look for other signs of CVA and TIA (transient ischemic attack).

3. *Associated with progressive dementia.* Inappropriate sexual behavior may occur due to two correlates of progressive dementia.

   a. Disinhibition. Loss of inhibiting brain functions similar to those found in CVA patients. Sexual behavior becomes inappropriate for the first time.

   b. Disorientation. Because of cerebral tissue loss and sensory losses, these patients may show inappropriate sexual behavior. However, it is important to note that this behavior is not *in itself* inappropriate, but may be a problem because of the time and place in which it is performed. For example, such a patient may masturbate in a lounge or dining room. Masturbation is hardly an inappropriate behavior in the absence of a suitable partner, but masturbation in the lounge *is* inappropriate.

4. *Intentional.* Patients who are less confused and able to function more independently may engage in inappropriate sexual behavior because it is part of their behavioral history. Genital exposure, public masturbation, fondling, sexual contacts with incompetent and defenseless partners, and other forms of sexual behavior are as likely to occur in geriatric facilities as in any other place in society.

Strategies to Manage Inappropriate Sexual Behavior

These techniques have been used successfully to manage inappropriate sexual behavior. We have circled the number(s) of the methods used with the client to cope with such behavior in the past.

1. *Observation.* Close observation of the inappropriate sexual behavior is essential and should include the setting in which the behavior occurred, the nature of the behavior, target of the behavior, time of day, level of disorientation, and immediate consequences for the client and others in the environment. This information is needed to determine the category of sexual behavior involved and which strategy is to be implemented. Try to keep your personal value judgments and preconceived ideas about "appropriate" behavior out of the observations. The information should help you determine the type of behavior that is appropriate for each client.

2. *Drug modification.* This method can be used for inappropriate sexual behavior induced by medication. For dystonia, note if the behavior occurs in the absence of others (i.e., sitting, lying down, walking). The physician may consider reducing the medication, dosing singly at bedtime, or changing to another medication.

3. *Limiting access.* This technique is used predominantly with Categories 3 and 4 above. For confused or disinhibited patients, you might decrease the likelihood of unfortunate sexual contact or embarrassment by moving the patient from one room to another, changing roommates, placing the person in a private room, changing to a same-sex aide, or limiting public outings. Though the level of confusion may increase after such changes, the problem may be partially resolved if the target person is not available or made to feel uncomfortable.

   This behavioral technique is the first step applied to clients exhibiting Category 4 behavior, at least until Strategy 5 below can be implemented. However, if the client continues the problem behavior even after Strategy 5 has been attempted, a more structured or restricted placement may be necessary.

4. *Stimulus control.* This method is used primarily with clients exhibiting Categories 1b, 3a, and 3b behavior. Confused patients simply may not realize that the setting is inappropriate for the behavior. The lounge or dining room may look the same to them as their own rooms.

   It may be necessary to use large, colorful cues in the client's own room signifying the behavior is permitted there. Use a single bright color, not a written sign, above the client's bed for best results. At the same time, discourage (by interrupting or light restraint) the same behavior in other, more public areas.

When the behavior occurs, take the patient before the activity is completed into his own room, point to the color cue, and allow the behavior to continue. By following this procedure every time the behavior occurs in the wrong setting and allowing it to continue in the private setting, the exposure or masturbation should begin to occur only in the designated area(s).

5. *Limit-setting and selective reinforcement.* This behavioral technique is used with Category 4 behavior. Tell the client gently but firmly that the behavior you have observed cannot be allowed to continue at your residence. If this warning fails, tell the client you will have to remove certain privileges (e.g., television, favorite foods, cigarettes, outings, craft classes, and the like) the next time the behavior occurs. Make sure that the behavior is truly intentional and not the result of drug-induced confusion or disinhibition. Punishing behavior that is not under the client's control leads to frustration and sometimes aggression.

When the client is not engaging in the targeted behavior, give the client reinforcement (e.g., sit and talk, provide a favorite food or item, and the like). This approach increases the level of appropriate behavior and reduces the likelihood that another type of inappropriate behavior will arise to replace the targeted sexual activity.

We hope that this discharge program will help in your management of this client. Please keep in mind that it is extremely important before applying any of the behavioral techniques to determine the correct category of behavior for the client. If you have any doubts, it is probably better not to use Strategy 5, since it will unduly upset an already disoriented or confused client.

If you have any questions regarding the client or the techniques described in this program, please call us.

References

Atthowe, J. M. (1972). Controlling nocturnal eneuresis in severely disabled/chronic patients. *Behavior Therapy, 3*, 232–239.

Ayllon, T., & Michael, J. (1959). The psychiatric nurse as a behavioral engineer. *Journal of the Experimental Analysis of Behavior, 2*, 323–334.

Bakos, M., Bozic, R., Chapin, D., & Neuman, S. (1980). Effects of environmental changes on elderly residents' behavior. *Hospital and Community Psychiatry, 31*, 10, 677–682.

Baltes, M. M., & Barton, E. M. (1977). New approaches toward aging: A case for the operant model. *Educational Gerontology: An International Quarterly, 2*, 383–405.

Baltes, M. M., Burgess, R. L., & Stewart, R. B. (1980). Independence and dependence in self-care behaviors in nursing home residents: An operant observational study. *International Journal of Behavioral Development, 3*, 489–500.

Baltes, M. M., Honn, S., Barton, E. M., Orzech, M., & Lago, D. (1983). On the social ecology of dependence and independence in elderly nursing home residents: A replication and extension. *Journal of Gerontology, 38*, 556–565.

Baltes, M. M., & Zerbe, M. B. (1976a). Reestablishment of self-feeding in a nursing home resident. *Nursing Research, 25*, 1, 24–26.

Baltes, M. M., & Zerbe, M. B. (1976b). Independence training in nursing home residents. *The Gerontologist, 16*, 428–432.

Barton, E. M., Baltes, M. M., & Orzech, M. J. (1980). Etiology of dependence in older nursing home residents during morning care: The role of staff behavior. *The Journal of Personality and Social Psychology, 38*, 423–431.

Birren, J. E. (1970). Toward an experimental psychology of aging. *American Psychologist, 25*, 124–135.

Blackman, D. K. (1977, December). *Control of urinary incontinence among the institutionalized elderly.* Paper presented at the meeting of the Association for the Advancement of Behavior Therapy, Atlanta, GA.

Blackman, D. K., Howe, M., & Pinkston, E. M. (1976). Increasing participation in social interaction of the institutionalized elderly. *The Gerontologist, 16,* 69–76.

Boczkowski, J. A. (1984). Biofeedback training for the treatment of chronic pain in an elderly arthritic female. *Clinical Gerontologist, 2,* 3, 39–46.

Bonner, C. D. (1969). Rehabilitation instead of bedrest? *Geriatrics, 24,* 109–118.

Brink, T. L., Yesavage, J. A., Lum, O., Heersema, P., Adey, M., & Rose, T. L. (1982). Screening tests for geriatric depression. *Clinical Gerontologist, 1,* 37–43.

Bruning, R. H., Holzbauer, I., & Kimberlin, C. (1975). Age, word imagery, and delay interval: Effect on short-term and long-term retention. *Journal of Gerontology, 30,* 312–318.

Burgio, K. L., Whitehead, W. E., Engel, B. T., & Middaugh, S. J. (1984, November). Behavioral treatment of urinary incontinence in elderly men and women. In S. R. Rapp (Chair), *Health, behavior, and the elderly.* Symposium conducted at the meeting of the Association for the Advancement of Behavior Therapy, Philadelphia, PA.

Cummings, I., Benson, D. F., & LoVerne, S. (1980). Reversible dementia: Illustrative cases, definition and review. *Journal of the American Medical Association, 243,* 23, 2434–2439.

Davies, R. K., Tucker, G. J., Harrow, M., & Detre, T. D. (1971). Confusional episodes and tricyclic antidepressant medication. *American Journal of Psychiatry, 128,* 95–99.

D'Zurilla, T. J., & Goldfried, M. R. (1971). Problem solving and behavior modification. *Journal of Abnormal Psychology, 78,* 107–126.

Eastwood, M. R., & Corbin, S. (1983). Hallucinations in patients admitted to a geriatric psychiatry service: Review of 42 cases. *Journal of the American Geriatric Society, 31,* 593.

Erber, J., Herman, T. G., & Botwinick, J. (1980). Age differences in memory as a function of depth of processing. *Experimental Aging Research, 6,* 341–348.

Ernst, P., Beran, B., Safford, F., & Kleinhauz, M. (1978). Isolation and the symptoms of chronic brain syndrome. *The Gerontologist, 18,* 5, 468–473.

Feldman, H. S., & Lopez, M. A. (1982). *Developmental psychology for the health care professions. Part 2: Adulthood and aging.* Boulder, CO: Westview Press.

Ferster, C. B. (1965). Classification of behavioral pathology. In L. Krasner & L. P. Ullman (Eds.), *Research in behavior modification.* New York: Holt, Rinehart & Winston.

Foxx, R. M., & Azrin, N. H. (1973). *Toilet training the retarded: A rapid program for day and nighttime independent toileting.* Champaign, IL: Research Press.

Freeman, F. R., & Rudd, S. M. (1982). Clinical features that predict potentially reversible progressive intellectual deterioration. *Journal of the American Geriatric Society, 30,* 449–451.

Geiger, G. O., & Johnson, L. A. (1974). Positive education for elderly persons, correct eating through reinforcement. *The Gerontologist, 14,* 488–491.

Girardeau, F. L., & Spradlin, J. E. (1964). Token rewards in a cottage program. *Mental Retardation, 4,* 2, 345–351.

Goldfried, M. R., & Davidson, G. C. (1976). *Clinical behavior therapy.* New York: Holt, Rinehart & Winston.

Goldfried, M. R., & Sprafkin, J. N. (1974). *Behavioral personality assessment.* Morristown, NJ: General Learning Press.

Haley, W. E. (1983). Behavioral self-management: Application to a case of agitation in an elderly chronic psychiatric patient. *Clinical Gerontologist, 1,* 3, 45–52.

Hanley, I. G. (1981). The use of signposts and active training to modify ward disorientation in elderly patients. *Journal of Behavior Therapy and Experimental Psychiatry, 12,* 241–247.

Hicks, R., Dysken, M. W., Davis, J. M., Lesser, J., Ripeckyj, A., & Lazarus, L. (1981). The pharmacokinetics of psychotropic medication in the elderly: A review. *Journal of Clinical Psychiatry, 42,* 374–384.

Hoyer, W. J. (1973). Application of operant techniques to the modification of elderly behavior. *The Gerontologist, 13,* 18–22.

Hoyer, W. J. (1975). Problem behaviors as operants: Applications with elderly individuals. *The Gerontologist, 15,* 452–456.

Hoyer, W. J., Kafer, R. A., Simpson, S. C., & Hoyer, F. W. (1974). Reinstatement of verbal behavior in elderly mental patients using operant procedures. *The Gerontologist, 14,* 149–152.

Hunt, J. G., Fitzhugh, L. C., & Fitzhugh, K. B. (1968). Teaching "exitward" patients appropriate personal appearance by using reinforcement techniques. *American Journal of Mental Deficiency, 73,* 41–45.

Hussian, R. A. (1981). *Geriatric psychology: A behavioral perspective.* New York: Van Nostrand Reinhold.

Hussian, R. A. (1982). Stimulus control in the modification of problematic behavior in elderly institutionalized patients. *International Journal of Behavioral Geriatrics, 1,* 33–42.

Hussian, R. A. (1984). Behavior therapy in geriatrics. In J. P. Abrahams & V. Crooks (Eds.), *Geriatric mental health* (pp. 109–122). New York: Grune & Stratton.

Hussian, R. A., & Davis, R. L. (1983, May). *Analysis of wandering in institutionalized geriatric patients.* Invited paper presented at the meeting of the Association for Behavior Analysis, Milwaukee, WI.

Hussian, R. A., Hill, S. D., & Ward, R. T. (1982). Assessment of drug-induced abnormal motor movements in institutionalized elderly patients. *International Journal of Behavioral Geriatrics, 1,* 47–55.

Hussian, R. A., & Yore, B. (1984, November). *Application of behavioral programming on a Texas State Hospital geriatric unit: Procedures and outcome.* Paper presented at the meeting of the Gerontological Society of America, San Antonio, TX.

Jeffers, F. C., & Nichols, C. R. (1961). The relationship of activities and attitudes to physical well-being in older people. *Journal of Gerontology, 16,* 1, 67–70.

Jones, E. A., Brown, K., Noah, J. C., Jones, D. A., & Brezinski, W. (1977, December). *Three behavioral strategies to increase participation in leisure time activities in institutionalized geriatric populations.* Paper presented at the meeting of the Association for the Advancement of Behavior Therapy, Atlanta, GA.

Kleitsch, E. C., Whitman, T. L., & Santos, J. (1983). Increasing verbal interaction among elderly socially isolated mentally retarded adults: A group language training procedure. *Journal of Applied Behavior Analysis, 16,* 217–233.

Koncelik, J. A. (1976). *Designing the open nursing home.* Princeton, NJ: Van Nostrand Reinhold.

LeBray, P. R. (1979). Geropsychology in long-term care settings. *Professional Psychology, 70,* 475–484.

Lee, D., & Znachko, G. (1968). Training psychiatric aides in behavioral modification techniques. *Journal of Psychiatric Nursing and Mental Health Services, 6,* 7–11.

Lowenthal, M. F., & Zilli, A. (1969). *Colloquium on health and aging of the population.* Switzerland: S. Karger, A. G.

Lowenthal, N. (1958). Nobody wants the incontinent. *R. N., 21,* 82–85.

MacDonald, M. L. (1978). Environmental programming for the socially isolated aging. *The Gerontologist, 18,* 350–354.

MacDonald, M. L., & Butler, A. K. (1974). Reversal of helplessness: Producing walking behavior in nursing home wheelchair residents using behavior modification procedures. *Journal of Gerontology, 29,* 97–101.

Mace, N. L., & Rabins, P. V. (1981). *The 36-hour day: A family guide to caring with Alzheimer's disease, related dementing illnesses, and memory loss in later life.* Baltimore, MD: Johns Hopkins University Press.

McAllister, C. J., Scowden, E. B., & Stone, W. J. (1978). Toxic psychosis induced by phenothiazine administration in patients with chronic renal failure. *Clinical Nephrology, 10,* 191–195.

McClannahan, L. E., & Risley, T. R. (1974). Design of living environments for nursing home residents: Recruiting attendance at activities. *The Gerontologist, 14,* 236.

McClannahan, L. E., & Risley, T. R. (1975). Design of living environments for nursing home residents: Increasing participation in recreation activities. *Journal of Applied Behavior Analysis, 8,* 261–268.

Melin, L., & Gotestam, K. G. (1981). The effects of rearranging ward routines on communication and eating behavior of psycho-geriatric patients. *Journal of Applied Behavior Analysis, 14,* 47–52.

Mueller, D. J., & Atlas, L. (1972). Resocialization of regressed elderly residents: A behavioral management approach. *Journal of Gerontology, 27,* 390–392.

Mueller, J., Hotson, J. R., & Langston, J. W. (1983). Hyperviscosity-induced dementia. *Neurology, 33,* 101–103.

Nigl, A. J., & Jackson, B. (1981). A behavior management program to increase social responses in psychogeriatric patients. *Journal of the American Geriatric Society, 29,* 92–95.

O'Quin, J. A., & O'Dell, S. (1981, November). *Increasing staff-resident interactions in a geriatric setting: "Real world" data.* Paper presented at the meeting of the Association for the Advancement of Behavior Therapy, Los Angeles, CA.

Parker, B., Deibler, S., Feldshuh, B., Frosch, W., Laureana, E., & Sillen, J. (1976). Finding medical reasons for psychiatric behavior. *Geriatrics, 31,* 87–91.

Paul, G. L. (1969). Chronic mental patients: Current status-future directions. *Psychological Bulletin, 71,* 81–94.

Peterson, R. G., Knapp, T. J., Rosen, J. O., & Pither, B. F. (1977). The effects of furniture arrangement. *Behavior Therapy, 8,* 464–467.

Philippopoulos, G. S. (1979). Psychodynamic approach to the most common psychiatric disorders in the elderly. *Psychotherapy and Psychosomatics, 32,* 241–248.

Pinkston, E. M., & Linsk, N. L. (1984). Behavioral family intervention with the impaired elderly. *The Gerontologist, 24,* 576–583.

Pollock, D. D., & Liberman, R. P. (1974). Behavior therapy of incontinence in demented inpatients. *The Gerontologist, 14,* 488–491.

Portnoi, V. A. (1980). T_3 toxicosis presented by depression in an elderly woman. *Postgraduate Medical Journal, 56,* 509–510.

Powell, L., & Courtice, K. (1983). *Alzheimer's disease: A guide for families.* Reading, MA: Addison-Wesley.

Quattrochi-Tubin, S., & Jason, L. A. (1980). Enhancing social interactions and activity among the elderly through stimulus control. *Journal of Applied Behavior Analysis, 13,* 159–163.

Quilitch, H. R. (1974). Purposeful activity increased on a geriatric ward through programmed recreation. *Journal of the American Geriatric Society, 22,* 226–229.

Rabins, P., Lucas, M. J., Teitelbaum, M., Mark, S. R., & Folstein, M. (1983). Utilization of psychiatric consultation for elderly patients. *Journal of the American Geriatric Society, 31,* 581–585.

Reisberg, B., Ferris, S. H., DeLeon, M. J., & Crook, T. (1982). The global deterioration scale for assessment of primary degenerative dementia. *American Journal of Psychiatry, 139,* 1136–1139.

Riege, W. H., & Inman, V. (1981). Age differences in nonverbal memory tasks. *Journal of Gerontology, 36,* 51–58.

Rinke, C. L., Williams, J. J., & Lloyd, K. E. (1978). The effects of prompting and reinforcement on self-bathing by elderly residents of nursing homes. *Behavior Therapy, 9,* 873–881.

Rosberger, Z., & MacLean, J. (1983). Behavioral assessment and treatment of "organic" behaviors in an institutionalized geriatric patient. *International Journal of Behavioral Geriatrics, 1,* 4, 33–46.

Sachs, D. A. (1975). Behavioral techniques in a residential nursing home facility. *Journal of Behavior Therapy and Experimental Psychiatry, 6,* 123–127.

Sanavio, E. (1981). Toilet retraining psychogeriatric residents. *Behavior Modification, 5,* 417–427.

Sanders, R. E., Murphy, M. D., Schmitt, F. A., & Walsh, K. K. (1980). Age differences in free recall rehearsal strategies. *Journal of Gerontology, 35,* 550–558.

Schnelle, J. F., Traughber, B., Morgan, D. B., Embry, J. E., Binion, A. F., & Coleman, A. (1983). Management of geriatric incontinence in nursing homes. *Journal of Applied Behavior Analysis, 16,* 235–241.

Seymour, D. G., Henschke, P. J., Cape, R. D. T., & Campbell, A. J. (1980). Acute confusional states and dementia in the elderly: The role of dehydration/volume depletion, physical illness and age. *Age and Ageing, 9,* 137–146.

Shraberg, D. (1980). An overview of neuropsychiatric disturbances in the elderly. *Journal of the American Geriatric Society, 28,* 422–425.

Sullivan, N. (1983). Vision in the elderly. *Journal of Gerontological Nursing, 9,* 228–235.

Task Force Sponsored by the National Institute on Aging. (1980). Senility reconsidered. *Journal of the American Medical Association, 244,* 259–263.

Thompson, L. W. (1976). Cerebral blood flow, EEG, and behavior in aging. In R. D. Terry & S. Gershon (Eds.), *Aging (Vol. 3): Neurobiology of aging.* New York: Raven Press.

Walsh, D. A., & Thompson, L. W. (1978). Age differences in visual sensory memory. *Journal of Gerontology, 33,* 383–387.

White, N. J. (1980). Complex visual hallucinations in partial blindness due to eye disease. *British Journal of Psychiatry, 136,* 284–286.

Winogrond, I. R., & Fisk, A. A. (1983). Alzheimer's disease: Assessment of functional status. *Journal of the American Geriatric Society, 31,* 780–785.

Woods, T. S. (1980). Bringing autistic self-stimulatory behavior under S-delta stimulus control. *British Columbia Journal of Special Education, 4,* 61–70.

Woods, T. S. (1983). The selective suppression of a stereotypy in an autistic child: A stimulus control approach. *Behavioural Psychotherapy, 11,* 235–248.

Yesavage, J. A., Brink, T. L., Rose, T. L., Lum, O., Huang, V., Adey, M., & Leirer, V. O. (1983). Development and validation of a geriatric depression screening scale: A preliminary report. *Journal of Psychiatric Research, 17,* 37–49.

Index

About the Authors

Richard A. Hussian, currently the Psychology Supervisor on the Geriatric Unit at Terrell State Hospital, Terrell, Texas, and Clinical Assistant Professor of Psychology at the University of Texas Health Science Center in Dallas, received his Ph.D. in Psychology from the University of North Carolina at Greensboro. He is author of the book *Geriatric Psychology: A Behavioral Perspective,* as well as numerous articles, chapters, and presentations on behavior therapy and geriatrics. He is a member of the Geriatrics and Gerontology Special Interest Group of the Association for the Advancement of Behavior Therapy and the Association for Behavior Analysis as well as the American Psychological Association, the Southeastern Psychological Association, and the Gerontological Society of America. His research interests include clinical gerontology, long-term care, correlates of organic mental disorders, and stimulus control techniques.

Ronald L. Davis is currently Unit Director of the Multiple Disabilities Unit of Terrell State Hospital. Prior to this he was Supervising Psychologist on the Geriatrics Unit where he implemented the first behavioral geriatrics program in a Texas psychiatric facility. He received his Ph.D. in Clinical Psychology from North Texas State University and has primarily been engaged in clinical work involving behavioral applications with diverse inpatient populations such as elderly persons, clients who are mentally retarded with accompanying psychiatric disorders, and clients who present severe behavior management problems. He is a member of the American Psychological Association, the Association for the Advancement of Behavior Therapy, and the Texas Psychological Association.